★READY-TO-GO MEETINGS

for Youth Ministry

Group Books

Loveland, Colorado

Ready-to-Go Meetings for Youth Ministry
Copyright © 1992 Group Publishing, Inc.

Edited by Michael Warden
Cover designed by Liz Howe
Cover illustrated by DeWain Stoll
Book designed by Dori Walker

ISBN 1-55945-168-8
11 10 9 8 7 6 5   03 02 01 00 99 98 97
Printed in the United States of America.

MY LIFE

MY FAMILY

MY RELATIONSHIPS

MY WORLD

When was the last time you felt rushed in planning a youth meeting for your kids? Two weeks ago? Last week?

Today?!

Here's your answer! *Ready-to-Go Meetings for Youth Ministry* packs together 70 hot meetings for youth groups—all set up and "ready to go!"

Each meeting outline includes a theme, scripture list, objective and instructions for quick preparation. Each meeting then takes you step by step through the meeting, with clear simple instructions and carefully constructed discussion questions to ask your kids. There are no handouts to bother with or difficult instructions to decipher. All you have to do is collect the supplies and go!

In addition to providing great time-saving features, these 70 meetings also provide spiritual truth that can really impact kids' lives. The meetings delve into important issues in creative, fun and active ways. Kids don't just hear the truth—they experience it! And they have fun at the same time.

For example, let your kids face their fears of violent crime by "kidnapping" the whole youth group ("Kidnapped!" page 137). Or get them to grapple with homelessness by pretending to be homeless themselves ("Hopeful Homeless," page 131). There are also meetings on personal life issues such as honesty and self-esteem, as well as meetings covering relationships of all kinds—with family, friends, even that "special someone."

Wherever your youth group is in its journey toward maturity in Christ, *Ready-to-Go Meetings for Youth Ministry* has meetings that can help them reach their goals. And with the easy-to-use format, you'll save yourself time and energy.

So go ahead and dive into the pages that follow. Enjoy this volume of active, meaningful meetings with your kids. You'll help build your kids' faith and make more time for yourself.

MY LIFE

THEME
Integrity

SCRIPTURE: Luke 16:1-12 and Psalm 15

OBJECTIVE: Challenge kids to do the right thing.

PREPARATION: For the meeting, you'll need a bag of miniature candy bars, a chair, a Bible and newspapers.

THE MEETING

1. TRAFFIC FLOW

Play Red Light, Green Light several times. During the game, one person stands facing the wall at one end of the room. The other players stand along the opposite wall. The person facing the wall calls out "green light," and the others run toward that person. When the person calls out "red light," everyone must stop moving. Then the person turns around and tries to catch players still in motion. If players are caught, they have to return to the start. The first player to touch the back of the person against the wall wins.

Afterward, ask: **How difficult or easy was it to stop when I called out "red light"? How did it feel when you were caught trying to get just a little farther? How did it feel when you weren't caught? How do some people in real life try to push the rules just a little further to get what they want?**

Say: **Today we're going to talk about integrity. Integrity is the art of doing the "right" thing. In the game we played, I played the role of someone looking for the right behavior. You were required to do the right thing even when I wasn't looking. Integrity is doing the right thing at all times—even when no one is looking.**

2. NO GAPS

Form two groups—a candy group and a guard group. Give the candy group a bag of miniature candy bars. Have the guard group form a circle facing out. Place a chair in the center of the circle. Have kids in the circle link elbows and guard the chair. The guards should not let the candy group touch the chair. Tell the candy group to try to lure the guards away with candy. Once a guard is lured away, the guard group cannot close the gap left by the missing member. The candy group members can then touch the chair. Once the chair is touched, the game is over.

After 10 minutes or after the chair is touched, ask: **How did you feel during this game? How easy or difficult was it to do your job? How easy or difficult was it to endure temptation?**

Read aloud Luke 16:1-12. Ask: **What is "a little thing" that you're required to be faithful in? What temptations do you face to stop being faithful in that thing? How do you endure those temptations? What "big thing" might God be using this little thing to train you for?**

3. GOOD AND BAD

Form groups of four. Give each group a newspaper. Have groups find in their newspapers one positive example of integrity and one negative example.

Have each group form a positive pair and a negative pair within itself. Have each pair choose one partner to take on the persona of the person from the newspaper; the other partner will interview this person. When pairs are ready, have them role play their interviews one at a time.

4. PRAYER OF INTEGRITY

Read this personalized version of Psalm 15 and have kids repeat each line after you: **Lord, how may I enter your holy tent? How may I live on your holy mountain? If my walk is innocent and I do what is right. If I speak truth from my heart and don't tell lies about others. If I do no wrong to my neighbor and do not gossip. If I withold respect from hateful people but I honor those who honor you. If I keep my promises even when it hurts. If I lend money without charge and don't take money to hurt innocent people. If I do these things, I will never be shaken. Amen.**

THEME
Miracles

SCRIPTURE: Exodus 14:21-31; Joshua 6:1-21; Matthew 9:1-8; Mark 7:24-30; Luke 6:6-11; John 9:1-7; and Acts 3:1-10

OBJECTIVE: Strengthen kids' faith to believe the incredible things God does.

PREPARATION: For the meeting, you'll need several copies of gossip magazines and Bibles. You'll also need unshelled peanuts, a Frisbee and a marker.

THE MEETING

1. WANTING TO KNOW

Form teams of four or fewer and give each team a copy of a gossip magazine. Tell kids you're going to hold a contest to find the "most believable" and the "most unbelievable" stories. Allow teams to search for several minutes and then have teams present their candidates.

Have kids vote on the most believable and the most unbelievable stories and congratulate the winning teams. Say: **Many things we read these days may or may not be true. But some incredible things are worthy of our belief. God is involved in our world today. We still experience his miracles and other great acts that build our faith.**

2. THE REAL McCOY

Form three groups and give each group a Bible. Have groups each find a Bible story describing a miracle. Offer these ideas: Exodus 14:21-31; Joshua 6:1-21; Matthew 9:1-8; Mark 7:24-30; Luke 6:6-11; John 9:1-7; and Acts 3:1-10.

Have groups each prepare a charade to help the rest of the class guess the miracle they found. After groups have presented their charades and identified the miracles, ask: **Why is this a miracle? Do you believe it really happened? Why or why not? If this miracle had happened yesterday somewhere in the world, would you believe it? Why or why not? What if it happened right in your own school or city?**

3. AMAZING BUT TRUE

Say: **To prove that incredible things happen today, I'm going to let you experience one right now. I have a miracle in my pocket right at this moment. I have something in my pocket right now that neither eye has seen nor hand has ever touched.**

Ask: **Do you believe me? Why or why not? If you do believe me, what do you think I have in my pocket?**

Allow kids a few minutes to guess and then pull from your pocket an unshelled peanut. Ask: **What do you think about my miraculous item? Why is the creation of a peanut— or any of God's gifts—a miracle?** (The peanut inside the shell wasn't created by human hands.) **How else can we see God's incredible working in our day-to-day lives?**

4. MIRACLE ROUND TABLE

Have kids form a circle. Then hold up a Frisbee on which you've written, "Round and round with miracles." Tell kids you're going to hold a round-table discussion about whether miracles still happen today like they did in Bible times. Pass the Frisbee around the circle as everyone says, "Round and round with miracles." The person holding the Frisbee when you finish the words answers this question: **Do miracles happen today? Why or why not?**

Pass around the Frisbee again as everyone says, "Round and round with miracles." Let another person answer the questions. Continue in this manner and ask other questions, such as: **What constitutes a miracle? Have you ever experienced a miracle today? Explain. Why might God decide to do miracles today? Why might God decide to stop?**

5. EVERYDAY MIRACLES

Give kids each an unshelled peanut and say: **Miracles come in all shapes and sizes. Let's close today by asking God to open our lives to miracles that surround us every day—even the simple ones like this peanut.**

Close with prayer. Encourage kids to take their unshelled peanuts home as reminders to believe the incredible and to notice miracles in day-to-day life.

12

THEME
God

SCRIPTURE: Deuteronomy 6:5; Psalm 55:22; 145:18; Proverbs 27:17; Matthew 6:33; 22:37-38; 1 Corinthians 16:13-14; and Ephesians 2:8

OBJECTIVE: Help kids center their lives on God.

PREPARATION: Use masking tape or ropes to form two concentric circles on the floor in the middle of the room. Make sure the innermost circle is about 5 feet across and that the outer circle is about 4 feet outside of the previous one. You'll also need paper plates and markers.

THE MEETING

1. PAPER PLATE TOSS

Form four teams. Give each team 10 paper plates. Ask the teams to each choose a team name that has the word "center" in it. Ask them to write their team name on their paper plates. Then have team members stand outside the outermost circle with their backs to the center and attempt to "center" their plates in the middle circle by tossing them over their heads.

Award 5 points to teams for each plate that lands in the center, 3 points for each plate partly in the center (but on a line) and 1 point for each plate completely inside the innermost ring. Award a prize to the team with the most points.

Ask: **Was it easy to center the plates without looking? Why or why not? Did you choose a method for getting your plates in the center circle or did you toss them blindly? What's at the center of your life? Do you blindly go from one activity to another, or do you try to focus on making a particular aspect of your life the center?**

2. WHAT'S AT THE CENTER?

Form groups of three or four. Give each group paper plates from the previous activity. Ask groups to brainstorm things that can be at the center of life, such as church, family, work, possessions, school, God and relationships. Have them write each idea on a paper plate.

3. WHERE'S YOUR CENTER?

Gather together. Have group members work together to determine where each plate should be placed in the circles to represent the priority it should have in their lives. Then, for each of the following questions, ask group members to stand next to the plate in the circles that best describes their answer. Ask: **Which activity do you spend the most time doing? Which do you think about the most? Which do you look forward to most? Which do you develop the most?**

4. CIRCULAR OBSERVATIONS

Have kids return to their small groups. For each of the previous questions, ask: **Where did most of the people stand? Why?**

Then ask: **How important is it to have God at the center of your life? What happens to your perspective and behavior if God is not at the center of your life?**

5. CENTERING ON THE BIBLE

Read aloud Deuteronomy 6:5; Matthew 6:33; 22:37-38; and 1 Corinthians 16:13-14. Ask: **How do you place God in the center of your life? What changes when God is at the center?**

Read aloud Psalm 55:22; 145:18; Proverbs 27:17; and Ephesians 2:8. Ask: **If you're off-center, how do you get back on-center?**

6. DAILY CENTERING

Give group members each a paper plate and ask them to draw concentric circles on their plates. Then, have them each write "My relationship with God" in the center of the circle. Ask group members each to tape their plate in a place where they'll see it each day. Close by squeezing everyone into the center circle on the floor. Have kids offer brief prayers asking God to help them to keep their focus on him.

THEME
God's Will

SCRIPTURE: Romans 12:1-2 and 1 Samuel 16:7

OBJECTIVE: Encourage kids to discover God's will for their lives.

PREPARATION: For the meeting, you'll need a bag of treats, a bowl of dirt, paper, pencils, envelopes and a Bible.

THE MEETING

1. HOT OR COLD

After kids arrive, pull aside one person and have him or her leave the room. Hold up a bag of treats and a bowl of dirt and have kids help you decide where to hide them. Once the items are hidden, form two groups. Tell one group to help the volunteer find the treats by calling out "warmer" or "colder" depending on how close the volunteer is to the bag. Have the other group distract the volunteer by trying to get him or her to find the bowl of dirt. Have that group also call out "warmer" or "colder" depending on how close the volunteer is to the bowl of dirt.

Call in the volunteer and tell him or her what you've hidden and what the rest of the group is going to do. Start the search. Once the volunteer has found one of the two items, stop the search and ask: **What was hard about this game? How did the volunteer know where to look? How did the volunteer decide who to listen to? How is this game like trying to discover God's will for your life? How does God use people around you to guide your life? How do you know who to listen to?**

2. A CHANCE TO DREAM

Form groups of four and give each person paper and a pencil. Have group members each draw a picture that represents at least one dream they have for their life. For example, kids might draw the White House or an astronaut. Once everyone has shared, ask: **Does God use your natural desires to direct you toward his will for you? Why or why not? Can we always depend on our desires to reflect God's will? Why or why not?**

3. THE DREAM WEAVER

Have a volunteer read aloud Romans 12:1-2. Then ask: **What does it mean to be a "living sacrifice"? What does it mean to "be transformed by the renewing of your mind"? Why are these things so important for discovering God's will for your life? What is God more concerned about: What you do with your life or who you become in your life? Explain.**

Read aloud 1 Samuel 16:7 and say: **Unlike people, who often measure success by what they do or how much money they have, God measures people from the inside out. So, although God does have a plan for what you should do or where you should go, his real concern is who you become. And he'll use whatever circumstances you're in to shape you into the person he wants you to be.**

4. LETTER TO MYSELF

Give each person a sheet of paper, a pencil and an envelope. Ask kids to think about the kinds of people they'd like to be in a year, based on Romans 12:1-2. Have kids each write themselves a letter describing that person. Ask volunteers to tell what they wrote. Then have kids seal their letters in the envelopes. On the envelopes, have kids write their names and "To be opened on (date one year from now)." Encourage kids to keep the letters in their Bibles so they won't misplace them before it's time to open them.

Form a circle and have kids offer sentence prayers, asking God to reveal his will for their lives—for what they're to do and who they're to become.

THEME
Fear

SCRIPTURE: 1 Samuel 17:1-50 and Psalm 18:2-3

OBJECTIVE: Encourage kids to face their fears by discovering God's faithfulness.

PREPARATION: For the meeting, you'll need newsprint, paper, pencils, a Bible, markers, a sheet of posterboard, construction paper, scissors, tape and small, smooth stones.

THE MEETING

1. WHAT'S MY LINE?

Ask for three volunteers. Secretly give each volunteer one of the following occupations: window washer, movie stunt person or lion tamer. Tell the other kids they have two minutes to ask yes-or-no questions of each volunteer to determine his or her occupation.

After two minutes, ask: **What do these occupations have in common?** (They're all risky or scary.)

Say: **Fears are a normal part of life for everyone, not just for people with scary occupations.**

2. TEARS AND FEARS

On newsprint list the following risky actions: eat or drink an unknown substance; stick your hand in a wiggling sack; walk across a deep stream on a log; ride a roller coaster; fly in an airplane; parachute out of an airplane; enter an unknown place by yourself; walk through a haunted house; accept a leadership position; face a big, strong, mean enemy; and make a public speech.

Give each person paper and a pencil. Ask them each to list the risky actions listed on the newsprint in order from "most fearful" to "least fearful." Then have kids tell about their lists. Ask for volunteers to tell about times they were frightened. Say: **In this meeting, we'll learn about how one teenager long ago handled fear.**

3. A GIANT FEAR

Form five groups (a group can be one person). Give each group a Bible, markers and a sheet of posterboard. Have each group create a mural that depicts 1 Samuel 17:1-50. Have groups tell about their murals.

Ask: **How did Goliath frighten the Israelites? Why did David feel confident he could meet the challenge of Goliath? How did God prepare David for this situation? Why did David not wear the protection offered by Saul? How did David feel standing before the giant?**

4. FEARFUL GREETING CARDS

Have kids stay in their five groups. Make sure each group still has a Bible. On newsprint, list the following ways to cope with a fear: identify the fear, know your strengths and weaknesses, trust God to help you face the fear, seek advice or help from others, and take action.

Assign each of the five groups one "coping with fear" principle and ask them to find specific verses in 1 Samuel 17:1-50 that illustrate their principle. Then have groups each read aloud their verse and tell about their principle.

Give kids paper and pencils. Ask kids to each write about a giant fear in their life. Then have them use the "coping with fear" list to write what steps they can take to overcome that fear. Encourage volunteers to tell about their fears.

Form pairs. Gives pairs each construction paper, scissors, markers and tape. Say: **Card shops today sell cards for every situation. What would a greeting card for someone who's afraid say? What would it look like? With your partner, design your own "fearful greeting card."**

Have pairs each tell about their greeting card. Give pairs each an envelope so they can send their card to someone.

5. GIANT SLAYERS

Read aloud David's words to Goliath from 1 Samuel 17:45. Say: **The power of God can remove fears from your life too. Just remember David and who he trusted to help him overcome his fears.**

Give kids each a marker and a small, smooth stone. Read aloud Psalm 18:2-3. Then have kids write "Psalm 18:2-3" on their stones. Urge them to keep their stones handy to remind them how to handle fears.

THEME
Time With God

SCRIPTURE: Psalm 95:6-7; Matthew 6:31-33; Luke 9:18-36; John 6:15; and 1 Timothy 2:1-8

OBJECTIVE: Help kids understand the importance of spending daily time with God.

PREPARATION: Set up four stations around the room. At the first station, have markers and paper. At the second station, have books teenagers might enjoy reading. At the third station, have pencils and paper. At the fourth station, have the recipe, ingredients and utensils necessary for baking cookies.

THE MEETING

1. A MINUTE HERE, MINUTE THERE

Form four groups. Explain the four stations. Say: **Each group will spend some time at each station and perform specific tasks. At station 1, you're each to draw a map of the United States. Draw as many states as you can. At station 2, you're each to read as much as you can of one of the books. At station 3, you're each to write a two-page story about what life might be like in the year 3000. At station 4, you're to make chocolate chip cookie dough**.

Assign each group its first station. Don't tell kids how long they'll have to do each activity. Explain that when you say "switch," each group is to move clockwise to the next station. Begin the activity. After no more than two minutes, call "switch." Do this four times so each group has a chance to be at each station. Then call time.

2. WHO HAS TIME?

Form a circle. Collect the beginnings of the maps, pictures and cookies. Ask: **Why aren't the activities complete? How did you feel as you tried to complete the activities at each station? Explain. How much time would it take to complete each activity? In order to complete tasks such as these, what kind of commitment do you have to** make? How is that commitment like the time you should spend developing relationships?

3. DEVELOPING RELATIONSHIPS

Form groups of no more than four. Give each group a clock or a watch. Then have group members each take one minute to learn as much as they can about the other kids in their group. After each group member has had a chance to get acquainted, distribute paper and pencils to each person. Have kids silently write down what they remember about the other kids in their groups. Then have them each take one more minute to ask questions or confirm the information on their paper.

Ask: **How much did you learn about each other in the first minute? Did you learn anything new in the second minute? Why or why not? What might you learn about each other if you had five minutes a day to spend talking together?**

4. GETTING TO KNOW GOD

Form pairs. Have partners read aloud Luke 9:18-36 and John 6:15. Say: **Just as we need to invest time to complete tasks, we need to invest time to get to know people. And taking time to get to know God should be our top priority.**

Ask: **Why did Jesus spend time alone with God? How might Jesus' ministry have been different if he hadn't spent time with God?**

Have partners read aloud Psalm 95:6-7; Matthew 6:31-33; and 1 Timothy 2:1-8. Ask: **What do these passages tell us about spending time with God? What are some ways we can spend time with God?**

5. GOD'S TIME

Have the group work together to finish making the cookie dough. Pray: **God, help us make time for you just as we make time for other parts of our lives. And help us make our time with you a priority. Amen.**

Then enjoy the sweet chocolate chip cookie dough.

THEME
Peace

SCRIPTURE: Genesis 37:1-11; 1 Kings 19:1-8; Psalm 23; and Acts 16:16-40

OBJECTIVE: Help kids find God's peace in the middle of the world's stress.

PREPARATION: For this meeting, you'll need newsprint, tape and a marker.

THE MEETING

1. STRESSED OUT

Form a circle and ask a volunteer to sit in the middle. On "go," have everyone in the circle yell stressful messages at the person in the center. Suggest messages such as "Hurry up!"; "Watch out!"; "You'd better win!"; "Prejudice!"; "Homework due!"; "War!"; "No more money!"; and "Time to go!" After a minute, quiet everyone and ask the person in the center to talk about how he or she felt during the "stressful barrage."

Ask: **What causes teenagers to get stressed out?**

List kids' responses on newsprint taped to a wall. Ask kids to vote on the top five stressful situations in their lives and then circle those situations.

2. DISTRESSING SITUATIONS

Form three groups. Have each group read one of the following scripture passages: Genesis 37:1-11; 1 Kings 19:1-8; and Acts 16:16-40. Tell groups each to prepare a modern-day skit based on the story they read. The skits should identify the stress and how it was handled. Have groups each perform their skit. Then ask: **What caused stress in each situation? How did the people react to the stress? How did God provide peace during the stress?**

3. A PEACEFUL SOLUTION

Divide the three groups in half to form six groups. Assign each group a verse in Psalm 23 and ask them to paraphrase the verse to show how God provides peace. Have each group write its paraphrase on newsprint. Say: **God doesn't always remove our stress, but he does give us peace in the midst of stress.** Ask: **How does God bring peace during stressful situations?**

Talk about a time you felt God's peace during stress. Challenge kids to read Psalm 23 daily for a week, praying for God's peace.

4. MY STRESS

Form two equal circles of kids, one inside the other. Tell kids in each circle to face their counterpart in the other circle. Explain that you'll give the people in the outside circle 45 seconds to each complete a statement you'll read. After you call time, kids in the inside circle will each have 45 seconds to finish the same statement. After each statement, have kids in the outside circle rotate one person to the right. Read the following statements, and give kids time to respond.

- The time I feel the most stress is...
- When I'm stressed out I feel...
- One reason I have trouble finding God's peace is...
- To me, peace is like (choose one) a quiet stream, a sailing kite or a grand-slam home run, because...
- I wish I could give peace to...
- I need peace because...

5. A PROMISE OF PEACE

Form one circle. As you close in prayer, ask kids to call out one or two words that describe their stresses; for example, "homework" or "expectations." Thank God for his peace.

22

THEME
Worship

SCRIPTURE: Psalm 138; 146; and 147

OBJECTIVE: Open up to kids the meaning of worship and new ways to worship God.

PREPARATION: Create an altar using several scarves, a tablecloth, a podium or desk, and a 10×10-inch piece of posterboard. Tape the scarves around the posterboard. Write "ALTAR" on the posterboard as well. You'll also need Bibles and a person to lead the group in a worship song.

THE MEETING

1. GODS OF OUR OWN

Have kids each race to find something that represents the thing or person they love the most and bring it to a table at the front of the room; for example, car keys could represent a dreamed-about Ferrari or a photograph could represent an important relationship.

After kids have each placed an item on the table, choose representative items to place on the altar. As you place each item, ask kids why they love these things so much.

Then ask: **Is it possible to love these things too much? What does it mean to worship someone or something? Is it possible for someone or something other than God to become a god to us? Why or why not? When does something become a god to us?**

Say: **In Bible times, lots of people worshiped gods made by humans. Today it's really not much different. People worship cars, wealth, power and even other people. Today we're going to look at what real worship is.**

2. WERTENSNEER WORSHIP

Form groups of four. Give groups these instructions: **You've all decided Wertensneer is your god. The person in your group whose first name starts with the letter closest to W will be Wertensneer. The rest of you must decide on a list of four guide-**

lines for worship. For example, you may decide you must always stand if Wertensneer is sitting and sit if Wertensneer is standing. Or you can decide you may only speak in questions to Wertensneer. Be serious about this, because if you cross Wertensneer, he or she may zap you dead for the rest of the activity.**

Pull the Wertensneers aside and encourage them to be arrogant and demanding. However, warn them not to zap all their people.

Give groups each three minutes to worship their Wertensneer. Afterward, ask: **How did it feel to worship Wertensneer? Was he or she worthy of your worship? How does this kind of worship compare to the worship God wants from us?**

Say: **God wants our worship, and he truly deserves it. But he doesn't arrogantly demand it from us. And God won't zap us like Wertensneer did to some people. Let's see why.**

3. THE WHY OF WORSHIP

Form three groups. A group can be one person. Assign each group one of these psalms: Psalm 138; 146; and 147. Have each group use its psalm to write 10 guidelines for worshiping God.

Have groups each report the top five guidelines from their psalm. Then ask: **How do these verses make you feel? What do these verses say about who God is? What do they say about why we should worship God?**

4. REAL WORSHIP

Say: **There are lots of ways to worship God, most of which we can do either by ourselves or in a group. Some of the worship guidelines your group listed may be new or uncomfortable to you. We're going to worship God. As we worship, use some of the new guidelines you learned about worship.**

Have someone lead your group in a song of worship. Close with a prayer of praise to God.

THEME
Patience

SCRIPTURE: James 5:7-9
OBJECTIVE: Teach kids how to develop patience in their lives.
PREPARATION: On a sheet of newsprint, draw a diamond shape divided into seven sections. Cut apart the sections and write one of these words on each one: "parents," "friends," "dating," "yourself," "work," "school" and "siblings." You'll also need a deck of cards, a Bible and pencils.

THE MEETING

1. PATIENCE SYMBOL

Set out a deck of cards. Have kids work together to use the cards to create a symbol for the word "patience." For example, they could lay out the cards in a giant letter "P" or they could form a smiley face. Make sure each person gets a chance to add at least one card.

2. WHY BE PATIENT?

Read aloud James 5:7-9. Say: **Today we're going to talk about patience and how we can practice it in several areas in our lives.**

Ask: **Did you enjoy creating a symbol for patience? Why or why not? Why did that task require patience? Was it difficult to think of a symbol? Why or why not? Was it difficult to work with others? Why or why not? Why should we want patience in our lives? What areas of our lives require patience?**

3. VIRTUOUS JEWEL

Form seven groups. It's okay if a group is one person. Give each group a diamond section, but don't tell groups what shape the sections form when placed together. Give groups each a pencil and have them write on their section one way they could demonstrate patience in the area listed on their diamond section.

When groups are finished, have kids tell what they wrote about being patient with parents, friends, dating, themselves, work, school and siblings. Then have groups work together to re-create the diamond

25

shape on the meeting room floor. Ask: **How is patience like a jewel? What is its price? How is a patient person different from an impatient person?**

4. IT'S YOUR PLAY

Give each group member a pencil and a diamond from a deck of cards. If you have a large group, get enough card decks so everyone can have a diamond. Have kids write "Have patience" on their cards.

Remind group members of their ideas for being patient with family, friends and other situations in life. Encourage them each to tape their card to their bathroom mirror as a reminder to be willing to pay the price for the jewel of patience. Close with prayer.

THEME
Honesty

SCRIPTURE: Colossians 3:9-14
OBJECTIVE: Challenge teenagers to see the value of honesty.
PREPARATION: For the meeting, you'll need newsprint, a marker, tape, a Bible, paper and pencils. You'll also need a shoebox.

THE MEETING

1. TRUTH OR LIE?

Sit in a circle. Have kids each think of three "facts" others might not know about them. Tell them that none, one, two or all three things can be lies. One at a time, have kids tell their three "facts" and have the rest of the group guess how many (if any) are lies. Ask: **How does lying make you feel? Is it easy or hard for you to lie? Explain.**

2. HONESTY: THE BEST POLICY?

Form two groups of no less than three. Have groups each create two skits: one that shows a positive result of someone's honesty and one that shows a negative result of someone's dishonesty. Have groups each present their skits. Have kids briefly discuss each skit. Ask: **Is honesty always the best policy? Why or why not? When might honesty be inappropriate—if ever? Why do people lie? How do you feel when someone's been dishonest with you?**

3. COMMON LIES

Tape a sheet of newsprint to the wall. Have kids brainstorm situations when they've been tempted to lie. Write the situations on newsprint. Encourage them to be honest when they think of situations they've been in. Then have kids discuss why lies are common in each situation. Ask: **What keeps us from being honest all the time?**

4. HONEST DISCUSSIONS

Form pairs. Have partners discuss times they've felt uncomfortable being honest with someone.

Then have a volunteer read aloud Colossians 3:9-14. Ask: **Why does this verse say not to lie to one another?**

5. UNTRUTH'S CONSEQUENCES

Say: **Honesty isn't always easy. Sometimes, lying to a friend or a parent seems like an easy way out of a situation. But lies often come back to hurt people.**

Give teenagers each a sheet of paper and a pencil. Have them each write a covenant with God to work on being honest. Then have kids fold their papers and place them in a shoe box. Seal the box and promise the group it will stay sealed. Place it in a prominent place in your meeting room to remind kids to be honest.

Form pairs. Have partners take turns praying for each other. Encourage kids to work on being honest with one another and their families in the coming weeks.

THEME
Self

SCRIPTURE: Romans 12
OBJECTIVE: Lead kids toward a healthy, balanced view of themselves.
PREPARATION: Cut from magazines and newspapers several pictures of people who are familiar and unfamiliar to the kids. Get pictures with a variety of facial expressions. Write each one of these open statements on a separate strip of paper: "Nobody's better than me at...", "When it comes to...I'm the worst because...", "One of my many great abilities is...", "I will never be able to..." Place the strips in a paper sack. You'll also need paper, pencils, a Bible, a sheet of newsprint, a marker and tape.

THE MEETING

1. EGO MOVES

For each of the pictures, ask group members to respond in one of three ways to this question: How do you think this person views him- or herself?

Here are the responses: (1) as a fairly awesome person, stand up; (2) as only average, sit in a chair; or (3) as a rotten person, sit on the floor.

After going through the pictures, say: **How we see ourselves makes a big difference in how we relate to one another. But how do you know when you're out of balance in your view of yourself? Let's take a look at how we can develop a healthy self-image.**

2. EGO BAG

Form a circle. Pass the bag of statements around the group so everyone gets a statement to complete. Have the kids take turns completing their sentences to the person next to them.

Then ask: **What did these sentence-starters lead you to do? How**

29

did your sentence make you feel? Do you ever find yourself thinking of yourself in these ways? How do you feel if you do?

3. EGO MANNEQUINS

Give kids each a pencil and paper. Have a volunteer read aloud Romans 12. Then write Romans 12:3 on a sheet of newsprint and tape it to the wall. Form groups of four. Have groups each select one person to be their "ego-mannequin."

Say: **On "go," each group will take turns asking the mannequin of another group a question that will test whether the mannequin has a balanced self-image. Each group must tell its mannequin how to answer with body language alone. Your questions should help us see the kind of self-image the mannequins have; for example, "How do you feel when a friend wins an award you wanted?" Your mannequin's body language should reflect the kind of self-image described in Romans; for example, "I'm proud and happy for my friend."**

Give the groups three minutes to plan questions and then allow questioning to begin. After a few questions, ask: **How easy or difficult was it to give your mannequin a balanced self-image? How did Paul's advice from Romans help?**

4. BALANCED PRAYER

If you're close to a park with teeter-totters, take your group to the park for this closing. If you aren't near a park, have partners close with this prayer in your meeting room.

Form pairs. Have one partner write a brief prayer that asks God to help us love ourselves. Have the other partner write a brief prayer that calls on God to give us a healthy sense of modesty. Have pairs take turns on the teeter-totters praying their prayers.

THEME
Encouragement

SCRIPTURE: Acts 4:32-37; 9:23-27; and 11:22-30

OBJECTIVE: Help your kids become better encouragers.

PREPARATION: For the meeting, you'll need Kudos snacks, masking tape, 3×5 cards, pencils and Bibles.

THE MEETING

1. AWARD SHOW

Have kids stand up one at a time and let the group decide what an award for each person should be titled; for example, "best hair," "tallest boyfriend," "perfect attendance" or any other positive award. Make sure none of the awards are used as putdowns. After each award title is chosen, present to that person a Kudos snack.

After all the awards have been made, ask: **How did it feel to get your award? How does it feel to get recognized for something you've done well?**

Say: **People like to be encouraged, and we all need encouragement from time to time. Today we're going to talk about how we can be encouragers.**

2. BRIDGE

Tape two 5-foot lengths of masking tape on the floor, approximately 10 feet apart. Have kids stand behind one of the taped lines. Say: **The object of this exercise is for you to build a human bridge to get everybody across this 10-foot-wide river. But no more than three of you can touch the river. Once the bridge is built, the rest of you will have to cross the river without touching the ground.**

After the group has crossed, ask: **How did you feel as you built this bridge? Did anyone in particular encourage or support people as the bridge was built? If so, who? How did he or she encourage people? How are encouragers like bridges across tough times? How does it feel to actually be a bridge for others?**

3. WHAT A GUY!

Read aloud Acts 4:32-37; 9:23-27; and 11:22-30. After each passage, ask how it describes encouragement. Then ask: **What does it mean** when someone says, "A friend is someone who encourages you"? How do your friends encourage you? How do you encourage them? What does encouragement do for people?

4. BARNABAS ME

Say: **Even though he never really gets any credit for being a great leader in the Christian church, Barnabas stood by Paul when Paul needed him. Perhaps Paul couldn't have been as effective if it hadn't been for Barnabas' encouraging him from the background. When Barnabas encouraged people, they grew closer to the Lord. Think of someone who needs your encouragement to grow in his or her relationship with God.**

Close with a prayer for God to help kids each encourage the person they thought of.

THEME
Commitments

SCRIPTURE: Psalm 76:11; Ecclesiastes 5:4-7; and Matthew 1:18-25

OBJECTIVE: Challenge kids to keep commitments they make.

PREPARATION: For the meeting, you'll need red and orange suckers, paper, pencils and Bibles.

THE MEETING

1. SUCK IT UP!

Give kids each a red or an orange sucker. Distribute an even number of each color. Have kids mingle and talk to people with a different-colored sucker. As they mingle, have them complete this statement: "The toughest commitment I ever made and kept was..."

2. TO SIGN OR NOT TO

Say: **Today we're going to talk about making commitments and keeping them.**

Form two groups according to sucker colors—a red group and an orange group. Send the red group out of the room. Give each orange group member a sheet of paper and a pencil. Tell the orange group members that they'll each ask one person from the red group to sign to a commitment on a sheet of paper.

Tell them to each write their name at the top of the paper and the words "I commit" as a title on the page. Then ask them each to create a commitment for a person from the other group to commit to. Tell them to keep it simple, such as "Tie my shoelaces" or "Give me a shoulder rub." While they're writing, go to the red group.

Tell the red group that when they're asked to commit to a certain thing, they are each to say, "I commit." But when they are given the opportunity to sign their names, they can change their minds if they want to. Encourage at least half of the red group not to sign their names.

3. SIGN UP

Bring the red group back in the room. Have the red and orange groups line up facing each other. Have orange group members hold out their papers, read them and say, "Will you commit?"

Have red group members each say, "I commit." After some kids sign and some don't, ask: **How did you orange group members feel during this activity? How did you red group members feel? How easy or difficult was it to make a commitment and then not keep it? How did it feel when people promised to commit and then didn't? How did it feel when people kept their commitments?**

4. VOWS

Read aloud Matthew 1:18-25. Have kids call out things the townspeople might've said about Joseph's and Mary's situation. Ask: **If you had been Joseph, how would you have felt when your fiancee became pregnant by someone else? How difficult would it have been to keep your commitment to marry her? What does Joseph's keeping the commitment to Mary reveal about the kind of man he was?**

Say: **Commitments or promises can be difficult to keep. That's why we need to be very careful when we make commitments. Making commitments or vows is a serious thing to God.**

Have a volunteer read aloud Psalm 76:11 and Ecclesiastes 5:4-7. Ask: **How does God feel about our making vows? breaking vows? According to these verses, what should our attitude be when we make commitments to God?**

5. WATCH YOUR MOUTH

Say: **A commitment can be as simple as promising your mom that you'll take the trash out or as big as getting married. When we make commitments, people depend on us, and people are hurt if we break our commitments.**

Close in prayer, asking God to give kids wisdom when making commitments and the strength to follow through on their commitments.

34

THEME
God

SCRIPTURE: Exodus 17:8-16 and Romans 8:28-39

OBJECTIVE: Challenge kids to remember that God is in control, even when it seems he isn't.

PREPARATION: For the meeting, you'll need Bibles, paper, pencils and large erasers.

THE MEETING

1. OUT OF CONTROL?

Have kids stand in a group at arm's length from one another. Tell them they're all under your "remote control." When you point your finger in any direction, they must all immediately take two steps in that direction, stop and wait for a further "control signal."

After giving 10 remote-control signals, with kids responding, abruptly leave the room. Come back in two minutes and ask: **Who moved? Who just stood waiting for me to return? How did you feel when I controlled your actions? How were your feelings different when you had no directions? How is this experience like times when you've wondered whether God is in control of events in your life?**

Say: **The Bible tells us God is always in control, but sometimes that's hard to believe in tough situations. Let's look at an example of God's behind-the-scenes "remote control."**

2. MOCK BATTLE

Form two teams—Israelites and Amalekites. Then read aloud Exodus 17:8-16. Tell kids you're going to read verse 11 again, with long pauses between the two phrases: "As long as Moses held his hands up, the Israelites would win the fight" and "but when Moses put his hands down, the Amalekites would win." Say: **Without touching, act out this battle in slow motion. I'm Moses on the mountain-top, and you're the warriors.**

Read the first phrase and pause as you hold up your hands. Let kids have fun acting out the battle. Then read the second phrase, lower your hands and have the kids reverse the progress of the battle. Continue raising and lowering your hands for a few minutes.

IS GOD IN CONTROL?

Say: **In the real battle, the Israelites couldn't see Moses. All they knew was that sometimes they were winning and sometimes they weren't.**

Ask: **Have you ever felt like sometimes you're winning and sometimes you're not? Explain. How tough is it for you to believe that God is in control when it seems he's unware of your struggles?**

3. TOUGH TO SEPARATE

Have kids stay in their teams. This time, one team is the Worms, and the other team is the Fishers. The Worms tightly intertwine arms while the Fishers try to pull them apart. When a Worm is pulled away, he or she must help the Fishers. The activity is over when the Worms are all pulled apart or when two minutes are up. If any Worms are still together after two minutes, the Worms win.

Give each person paper and a pencil. Say: **Think about being held close to God and think about being separated from God. As I read Romans 8:28-39, the Worms will list things in this passage showing that God is always close to us. The Fishers will list things that can separate us from the love of God.**

Afterward, have volunteers each read their list.

4. NOTHING IS SOMETHING!

Say: **You Fishers found that nothing in "all creation" can separate us from the love of God. He's always close and in control.**

Have kids each use a pencil to list on the back of their paper something they think might cause God to abandon them—or at least love them less. Then give each person a large eraser as a gift. Tell kids to erase what they've written. Then close in prayer, thanking God for being in control and loving us at all times.

36

THEME
Jesus

SCRIPTURE: Isaiah 9:6-7; Jeremiah 23:5-6; Micah 5:2-5a; Matthew 11:3-6; 16:15-16; 21:6-15; Luke 23:39-43; and John 4:25-26, 42

OBJECTIVE: Help kids see that Jesus is more than just a friend—he's also the Messiah.

PREPARATION: Write each of the following words on separate 3×5 cards: cool, awe-struck, skeptical, excited, honored, shy and pushy.

For the meeting, you'll need newsprint, tape, markers, paper, pencils, Bibles and large metal nails. You'll also need these art supplies: paper clips, pipe cleaners, paper cups, yarn, aluminum foil and construction paper.

THE MEETING

1. VIP

Ask: **If a VIP came to our meeting, what would we need to do to get ready? Who would be here to greet this person? What makes a person a VIP?**

Have kids list the characteristics of a VIP on newsprint taped to a wall. Hand out the seven role-play cards to different kids. Ask kids with the cards to make believe a VIP is walking through the door; they should each act out the reaction—one at a time—listed on their card. Have the rest of the kids guess the reaction.

Write the following definition on newsprint as you say it. Say: **Jesus was a VIP when he came to earth. He was the long-awaited Messiah. The Messiah was the one anointed by God to save God's people and set up God's kingdom.**

2. EXPECTATIONS

Write the following scripture references on newsprint taped to a wall: Isaiah 9:6-7; Jeremiah 23:5-6; Micah 5:2-5a; Matthew 11:3-6; 16:15-16; 21:6-15; Luke 23:39-43; and John 4:25-26, 42.

JESUS THE MESSIAH

Form two groups and give kids each paper and a pencil. Make sure both groups have access to a Bible. Ask the first group to discover how the writers of the Old Testament viewed the Messiah by looking up the Old Testament references. Ask the second group to discover how the New Testament writers viewed the Messiah by looking up the New Testament references. Have kids each write a résumé listing Jesus' qualifications and references as Messiah.

Have kids each present their résumé. Point out the differences between expectations and reality, referring back to the definition of "Messiah."

3. MESSIANIC LOGO

Tell kids to each design a symbol of Jesus as Messiah, using the art supplies listed in the preparation section.

After kids present their symbols, say: **Some people hang meaningful objects from their car rear-view mirrors. Where could you display this symbol to indicate what Jesus the Messiah means to you? Challenge kids to display their symbols during the coming week.**

4. UNDERSTANDING THE MESSIAH

Give kids a long nail to hold while they sing a favorite song about Jesus. After the song, say: **The nail you hold is a symbol of Jesus' mission as Messiah—he died to save us all. Take your nail home and put it in a prominent place as a daily reminder of God's love for you.**

Close by asking kids to each offer a one-word prayer of praise or thanks for Jesus the Messiah.

THEME
Life

SCRIPTURE: Proverbs 16:20; Philippians 4:19; and 1 John 3:1-3

OBJECTIVE: Help kids learn to enjoy life.

PREPARATION: Fill the room with lots of balloons, streamers, confetti and other party decorations. Make it as cheery and bright as possible. Have upbeat party music ready to play.

For the meeting, you'll need blindfolds, a Bible and markers.

THE MEETING

1. DOWN AND OUT

As kids arrive, blindfold them before they see the brightly decorated meeting room. Lead kids into the room and help them find seats.

Begin the meeting by asking kids to describe times they've felt down or depressed. Ask them to share things that happened during the past week that made them feel angry or frustrated. Then start to play the party music quietly in the background.

2. LIFE CAN BE GREAT!

Ask: **What's the opposite of depression or anger? What's one thing that adds real joy to your life?**

Read aloud Proverbs 16:20; Philippians 4:19; and 1 John 3:1-3.

Ask: **How do these scriptures make you feel? How can they help you find joy in life?**

3. BRIGHT LIFE

Turn up the music and have kids take off their blindfolds. Have them each say one word that describes how they feel about the decorated room. After kids each say one word, form groups of no more than four. Have groups brainstorm five things they can do to love life more. Then have groups present their ideas to the other groups. If possible, do some of the ideas right away.

4. GIFT OF LIFE

Have kids spend one or two minutes batting balloons around the

LEARNING TO LOVE LIFE

room while the music plays. Challenge them to work together to try to keep all the balloons from touching the floor.

When the time is up, say: **God gave each one of us a wonderful life to live. Just as the simple joy of playing with balloons can help us feel good about ourselves, learning to love God more can help us love life more, too.**

Form pairs. Have pairs each grab two balloons. Pass out markers. Have kids each write one thing they appreciate about their partner on a balloon and then give that balloon to their partner. Encourage kids to take their balloons home as a reminder to love life.

Close the meeting by having kids each offer one-word prayers of thanks to God for the gift of life.

THEME
Decision-making

SCRIPTURE: Daniel 1.3-19

OBJECTIVE: Challenge teenagers to see how important God is in their decision-making processes.

PREPARATION: Read Daniel 1:3-19. Then write each of the following questions on a separate 3×5 card: What was the problem? What were the risks or benefits if Daniel didn't obey the king? What were the risks or benefits if Daniel did obey the king? What did Daniel decide to do? How was God involved in Daniel's decision? What was the chief official's reaction to Daniel's decision? How did Daniel and the chief official compromise? What was the result of Daniel's decision? Why did Daniel stand by his decision?

For the meeting, you'll also need black paper, white paper, newsprint, masking tape, Bibles, a marker, pencils and a bag.

THE MEETING

1. BLACK OR WHITE?

Give each person one sheet of black paper and one sheet of white paper. Ask them to hold up the white paper if they agree with decision "a" or the black paper if they agree with decision "b." Read each of the following situations. Wait for responses after each situation.

Say: **You need to earn money for college. Would you: (a) take a low-paying job where you like the work and the people? or (b) take a high-paying job where you don't like the work and the people?**

Say: **Your friends tease you because your parents won't let you go to rock concerts. You win a free ticket from a radio station for a hot concert that's sold out. Would you: (a) lie to your friends and say you're going and then not go? or (b) lie to your parents** and say you're not going and then go?

Say: **Life sometimes gives us tough decisions to make. It's hard to know what to do.**

Ask kids to call out other tough decisions they've had to make. List those decisions on newsprint taped to a wall.

2. A TOUGH DECISION

Have kids make a large Tic Tac Toe board on the floor with masking tape. In each square, place one of the 3×5 cards with a question face down. Form two teams and read aloud Daniel 1:3-19. Then have teams play Tic Tac Toe. Teams must each answer their chosen square's question before they're awarded an X or O. Play until one team wins or all questions are answered.

3. A DECISION-MAKING PLAN

Using the Tic Tac Toe questions, ask kids to make a list of decision-making steps. List the steps on newsprint.

Ask: **How can God help you make a decision? How can God use people, events and scripture to guide you? How do Christians often close God out of the decision-making process?**

Pass out pencils and have kids each write in their Bible the decision-making steps as a reference for future decisions.

4. TOUGH DECISIONS

Form groups of no more than five. Give each group paper. Tell them each to make up a "Tough-Decision Case Study" based on real decisions others have had to make. Have each group pass its case study to another group. Ask groups to each solve the problem using the decision-making steps. Ask groups to each present their solution.

5. MY DECISION

Give each person paper and a pencil. Tell kids each to write a tough decision they face. Keep these anonymous. Place papers in a bag. Have kids each pull out a paper and commit to pray for that decision during the week. Close by asking God's guidance in making the tough decisions of life.

THEME
Christian
Growth

SCRIPTURE: Psalm 34:19; 51:16 17; 55:22; Luke 9:62; Luke 22:54-62; John 3:16; Romans 2:9-10; 1 Corinthians 10:24; Ephesians 2:8; Philippians 1:29; James 2:15-16; 1 Peter 4:12-16; and 5:8-10.

OBJECTIVE: Help kids understand that Christian growth often comes through trials and hard experiences.

PREPARATION: For the meeting, you'll need a watermelon and a honeydew melon. You'll also need a small trophy, watermelon-color construction paper, brown construction paper, newsprint, tape, markers and Bibles.

THE MEETING

1. WATERMELON CONTEST

Form teams of three or more. Give each team an ample supply of watermelon. Tell teams they'll be competing to see which one can eat all of its watermelon first—without eating the seeds. Just before you start the contest, replace one team's watermelon with slices of honeydew, cantaloupe or another melon with seeds removed.

On "go," have teams consume their melons. Award the winning team a small trophy. Ask: **How did you feel when I gave one team an easier-to-eat melon? Were you frustrated that you had to slow down for the seeds? Why or why not?**

2. WATERMELON CHRISTIANS

Say: **Being a Christian is like eating a watermelon. Even though you enjoy the fruit, the seeds are an inconvenience and a trial. But just as seeds are necessary for growth, our trials are necessary for Christian growth.**

Form two groups. Give one group watermelon-color construction paper and the other group brown construction paper. Ask the "watermelon" group members to tear their construction paper into many watermelon shapes, then list what's great about being a Christian on them. Have the "brown" group tear seed-shape pieces of construction paper and list what's tough about being a Christian on them.

Form a circle and place all the "watermelon" and "seeds" in the center. Ask: **Why are there negative aspects of the Christian life? What would we be like if everything was positive? negative?**

3. THE GOOD AND THE BAD

Tape two sheets of newsprint onto a wall. Write "Good Stuff" on the top of one and "Not-So-Good Stuff" on the top of the other. Then have volunteers take turns reading aloud the following scripture passages. After each one is read, ask the group to vote on whether the passage represents a good, or not-so-good, aspect of Christianity. Write a key phrase or word on the appropriate newsprint.

Here are the scriptures: Psalm 34:19; 51:16-17; 55:22; Luke 9:62; John 3:16; Romans 2:9-10; 1 Corinthians 10:24; Ephesians 2:8; Philippians 1:29; James 2:15-16; and 1 Peter 4:12-16.

4. GROWTH ISN'T ALWAYS FUN

Have kids each choose a partner. Ask partners to take turns telling about a time something painful happened to them and how they grew through that experience.

After five or 10 minutes, read aloud Luke 22:54-62. Ask: **How do you think Peter felt after this experience? Explain. Did his faith grow or weaken after this event? How do you normally react to difficult situations? Based on the scriptures read earlier, what's the Christian life supposed to be like?**

5. MUTUAL SUPPORT

Combine two sets of partners to form small groups. Ask group members to read together 1 Peter 5:8-10 and then kneel holding hands in a small circle. Have them each pray for God's help to grow through the tough times.

Have each person grab a construction-paper watermelon or seed and take it home as a reminder that growth often comes through adversity.

44

THEME
Christian Growth

SCRIPTURE: Exodus 20:17; Matthew 7:13-14, 16, 24-27; Mark 8:38; Luke 14:27-35; Romans 12:2; 1 Corinthians 10:24; James 1:19-20; and 4:8

OBJECTIVE: Challenge teenagers to learn spiritual discipline as a way of life.

PREPARATION: Ask kids to bring to the meeting large suitcases filled with books or other heavy items. Have kids set up a complicated obstacle course using objects available in your meeting room. You'll also need Bibles, a clock or watch with a second hand, a prize for the opener, a cassette player and Russ Taff's self-titled cassette, newsprint, tape and markers.

THE MEETING

1. NARROW WAY

Form teams of no more than five. Show teams the obstacle course. Explain that each team will compete for the best time. Say: **I'll add up the individual times for each team member to determine the total time for each team. The team with the lowest total time wins a prize.**

Have the first person on each team run the course. Record the time for each participant. Then hand weighted suitcases to kids on one or two teams.

Say: **For the next rounds, some kids will be required to carry heavy suitcases through the course. If the suitcases are put down at any time, a 10-second penalty will be assessed.**

Teenagers will complain about the unfair competition, but continue until all teams have finished the race. Award a prize to the winning team.

2. EXCESS BAGGAGE

Form a circle and ask: **Was the race fair? Why or why not? If you had to carry luggage, how did you feel? If you didn't have to carry luggage, how did you feel as you watched those who did?**

Form groups of no more than four. Have groups each read Matthew 7:13-14. Ask: **What does this passage mean? How is the narrow gate like our obstacle course?**

Read aloud Matthew 7:16, 24-27. Ask: **What kind of "baggage" makes it difficult to get through the narrow gate?**

3. INSIDE OR OUTSIDE?

Tape a long sheet of newsprint horizontally to the wall. Draw two parallel lines about 4 inches apart from left to right on the paper. Give kids each a marker.

Say: **When Jesus talked about the narrow gate, he implied that Christianity isn't something you can just "put on" like a coat. It requires spiritual discipline. Between the lines on the chart, write things we can do to develop our faith and love for God. Then list outside the lines things that pull us away from this discipline.**

Have volunteers read aloud the following scripture passages to spark ideas for the chart: Exodus 20:17; Mark 8:38; Luke 14:27-35; Romans 12:2; 1 Corinthians 10:24; James 1:19-20; and 4:8. Then give teenagers 10 to 15 minutes to list their ideas on the chart.

4. WALKING BETWEEN THE LINES

Have kids look at the chart. Ask them to each think about times they're outside the lines each day. Then have kids each find a quiet place in the room and pray silently for strength to walk between the lines.

5. NARROW PATH

Form a circle. Place the suitcases from the opening activity in the center. Say: **Walking between the lines isn't always easy. As you can see on the wall chart, there are many kinds of "baggage" that can get in our way. But with God's help, and one another's encouragement, we can stay on the narrow path as we pursue a relationship with God.**

Play Russ Taff's song "Walk Between the Lines" to close.

THEME
Suffering

SCRIPTURE: Mark 15:15-32; Romans 5:3-5; and 1 Peter 4:12-19

OBJECTIVE: Give suffering a place of honor in your kids' lives.

PREPARATION: Make a 6- to 12-inch-long figure of a human being out of modeling clay. You'll also need straight pins, pushpins, rubber bands, Bibles, newsprint, markers, 3×5 cards and pencils.

THE MEETING

1. PICKING CHERRIES

Have kids stand with their arms straight out at their sides, without touching anyone, and flex their fingers as though they're picking cherries from trees on either side of them. Don't allow kids to bend their elbows or let their arms droop. Right away ask: **This isn't too tough, is it?**

Within a couple of minutes, kids will begin to drop their arms from the pain of holding them up. When all the kids have let their arms drop or droop, ask: **Why did you drop your arms? How is the weariness you feel like suffering? How is continuing to hold up your arms like perseverance?**

Say: **You've experienced a bit of suffering. Today we're going to learn about one kind of suffering, what it means in our lives, why we experience it and what it can do for us.**

2. FOR US

Set the clay figure, straight pins, pushpins and rubber bands on a table. Say: **When we think of suffering in the Bible, we most often think of the suffering Jesus did for us.**

Assign each kid a different verse from Mark 15:15-32. It's okay if kids have more than one verse or the same verse. Say: **This clay figure represents Jesus. We're going to do to this Jesus some of what was done to him when he was here on earth.**

Encourage kids to take this seriously and imagine the clay figure really is Jesus as the activity proceeds.

Read through the passage twice. Have kids listen the first time. The

47

second time, have kids each do to the clay-figure Jesus what their assigned verse says.

Then ask: **How did you feel as you saw what the clay Jesus went through? How did you feel as you made the clay Jesus suffer? How is this similar to or different from what the real Jesus endured? Why did Jesus have to go through such suffering?**

3. FOR HIM

Ask: **What kinds of suffering do we experience today because of following God?**

List kids' answers on newsprint. Work with kids to narrow the answers to the top three sufferings they experience; these should be sufferings everyone has experienced.

Form three "suffering" groups. Have kids get in the suffering group that characterizes the suffering they feel most strongly as a Christian. Have groups each read aloud Romans 5:3-5 and 1 Peter 4:12-19.

In their groups, have kids discuss the following questions: **What good is the suffering we go through? What does it mean to "participate in the sufferings of Christ"? According to these scriptures, what motive do we have for willingly suffering for our faith?**

4. FOR ME

Give each person a 3x5 card and a pencil. On one side, have them each write the quality they'd most like to possess. On the other side, have them each write their own commitment to God to endure suffering for him.

Encourage kids to take the cards home and post them where they'll see them daily. Close by thanking God for the ways kids will benefit from the suffering they'll go through in living for him.

THEME
Appearance

SCRIPTURE: Matthew 6:25; 6:28; 6:31-33; and Luke 12:22-23

OBJECTIVE: Help kids shift their focus from outward appearances to inward qualities.

PREPARATION: String a clothesline across the meeting room. You'll also need posterboard, 3×5 cards, pencils, newspapers, straight pins and construction paper, Bibles, markers, scissors and tape.

THE MEETING

1. OFFICIAL INITIAL

Ask: **What kinds of clothes do you like to wear?**

Have kids each respond by saying types of clothes that start with their initials. For example, Carli Hart could say, "colorful hats" and David Smith could say, "dark shoes." Make the game extra tough by asking kids to remember each person's answers.

Say: **This meeting focuses on our outward appearances. Do clothes make a person? Why or why not?**

2. HAT-MAKERS AND MANNEQUINS

Form groups of no more than five. Give groups each some posterboard, a 3×5 card, a pencil, some newspapers, straight pins and construction paper.

Say: **Each group's task is to adorn one group member as a store mannequin in the latest, greatest hat style. You can use the supplies I gave you and anything else in the room.**

After their designs are complete, have groups each describe their creation by writing a "catalog description" of their hat on the 3×5 card.

Allow 10 minutes for the hat-makers to create their hats and catalog descriptions, then ask the mannequins to pose at the front of the room. Have the groups each read their catalog description. Then have kids vote on the hat that's the "hottest seller." Award the winning group all of the hats!

3. FASHION STATEMENTS

Have kids re-form their groups and discuss these questions:

49

Ask: **What does it mean when someone says, "You are what you wear"? Is this true today? Explain. Are clothes a status symbol? Why or why not? Why do some people base their self-worth on the clothes they wear? How can you avoid this tendency?**

4. YOU ARE WHAT YOU WEAR?

Give groups each a Bible. Assign each group one of the following verses to read aloud: Matthew 6:25; 6:28; 6:31-33; and Luke 12:22-23.

Then ask: **According to your verse, do clothes make a person special? Why or why not?**

5. CLOTHESLINE TIME

Give each person a sheet of construction paper, a marker and scissors. Ask kids to each cut out a shape of an article of clothing and write on it one thing they've learned. For example, "God looks at your insides, not your outsides" or "God doesn't care about the latest styles. God cares about who you are!"

Have kids each read aloud their advice. Then give kids each a piece of tape and have them tape their article of clothing to the clothesline.

6. HATS OFF TO YOU

Form a circle near the clothesline.

Say: **People used to congratulate each other by saying "Hats off to you!" Let's do the same thing by affirming each other's inner qualities.**

Place a hat on one person's head. Go around the circle and have each group member affirm that person's inner qualities by saying "Hats off to *(name)* because..." Make sure each person has a chance to wear the hat.

Close with prayer.

MY FAMILY

THEME
Parents

SCRIPTURE: Luke 2:39-51
OBJECTIVE: Challenge kids to find creative ways to appreciate their parents.
PREPARATION: For the meeting, you'll need newspapers, tape, a Bible, newsprint and a marker.

THE MEETING

1. OPENER: THANKLESS JOB

Form pairs. Give one partner in each pair newspapers and tape. Tell pairs to build the tallest creations they can with the supplies they have. But partners can't speak to each other. One partner must hold the supplies, and the other partner must do all the building. The supply-holding partner may dispense only one item at a time to the building partner.

Give pairs three minutes to complete their creations. Congratulate the winners. Ask the supply-holding partners: **How did it feel just holding the supplies and not being able to build or talk? How did it feel to be dependent on your partner but to not say any words of appreciation to him or her?**

Say: **Sometimes parents feel the same emotions the supply-holding partners felt. Good parents want to be involved in and give input to our lives, but they're seldom appreciated for what they do. During this meeting, we'll talk about how we can better understand and appreciate our parents**.

2. PARENTAL GIVEAWAY

Say: **We really care about one another here, right? Then this next activity shouldn't be too hard.**

Have kids each choose an item they have with them that's most important to them. When kids each have an item, have them find someone in the group to give it to. Make sure kids believe they're giving their items away for keeps. Each person may give and receive only one item.

Ask: **How did you feel giving away what was most precious to you? How were your emotions like the emotions parents feel when they slowly give up control of their kids' lives?**

Have kids return the items to their owners.

53

APPRECIATING PARENTS

Say: **Most parents do their best to raise their children. But some kids don't appreciate their parents' attempts. Now we're going to see what the Bible has to say about Jesus' relationship with his parents.**

3. EVEN PARENTS HAVE FEELINGS

Tell kids to think about Joseph and Mary's feelings as you read aloud Luke 2:39-51.

Read aloud the scripture and pause after each sentence. Have kids describe how Jesus' parents must've felt by giving a thumbs-up (they felt good) or a thumbs-down (they felt bad) signal whenever you pause.

Then ask: **Why did you choose the signals you did? How do Joseph and Mary's feelings compare with your parents' feelings when they're worried about you?**

4. WAYS TO SHOW WE CARE

Say: **At the end of the passage we just read, Jesus showed his appreciation to his parents by obeying them.**

Ask: **What are other ways to show parents appreciation?**

Have kids brainstorm a list of ideas for showing appreciation to parents. Encourage them to be creative; for example, offering to host a seasonal party for their parents and their parents' friends just to show appreciation. List their ideas on newsprint.

Close by having kids each thank God for their parents. Encourage kids to each choose one or two ideas and start showing more appreciation to their parents this week.

THEME
Confrontation

SCRIPTURE: Matthew 5:23-24; Matthew 18:15-17; and Galatians 6:1-5

OBJECTIVE: Help kids know when and how to confront their parents about personal issues.

PREPARATION: For the meeting, you'll need tape, newsprint, a marker and Bibles.

THE MEETING

1. PALM ATTACK

Form pairs and have partners stand about 2 feet apart, facing each other with palms out. Tell kids to plant their feet about a foot apart then try to knock their partners off balance using nothing but their palms against their partners' palms. Allow pairs several tries.

Then ask: **How did it feel to knock your partner off balance? How did it feel to get knocked off balance? How is this like confronting your parent about a problem? How is it different?**

Say: **When many people hear the word "confrontation," they immediately think about arguing with someone or trying to knock a friend "off balance" to make a point. But confrontation can be good. Let's see how.**

2. STOP THE FALL

Form groups of three and have kids take turns falling backward into the others' arms. Have fallers close their eyes and make their bodies stiff as they fall. Once everyone has fallen at least once, ask: **Did you enjoy this activity? Why or why not? How did it make you feel to fall backward? How did it make you feel to catch someone? Between this and the last activity, which is more like confronting your parent about a problem? Explain.**

Say: **Confronting family members can be a lot like catching them. When we see our relationship with our parents going in a direction that's bad for it, confronting your parents can be the most loving thing we can do.**

3. FACING THE ISSUE

Tape a sheet of newsprint to the wall and ask: **What kinds of issues would lead you to confront your parent(s)? How do you know**

55

when you should or should not confront your mom or dad? Write kids' responses on newsprint.

Then say: **It's sometimes hard to know when to confront someone. A good rule of thumb might be to confront family members when situations are potentially harmful to them, to you or to your relationship with them.**

Form three groups and give each group one of these passages: Matthew 5:23-24; Matthew 18:15-17; or Galatians 6:1-5. Have groups read their passages. Then ask: **What do these passages say about confrontation? How would these passages influence the way you presently relate to your family members?**

4. LEAN ON ME

Have kids form a circle and join hands. On "go," have the whole group slowly lean backward, relying on each other's grip to hold them up. Repeat the motion several times, then ask: **How does this circle symbolize our willingness to confront each other? If this circle were your family, could you lean back with them, too? Why or why not?**

Say: **As we've just experienced by leaning back in this circle, none of us can stand alone. We need each other to keep us from falling. And you and your family members need each other to keep from hurting yourselves, others or your relationships.**

Close with a prayer of thanks for each family represented in the room.

THEME
Fathers

SCRIPTURE: Exodus 20:12 and Ephesians 6:4

OBJECTIVE: Help kids understand and appreciate their fathers.

PREPARATION: A week before the meeting, ask teenagers to watch TV shows about families, such as *Growing Pains, The Cosby Show, Roseanne* or *Full House.* Then collect a supply of clothes a dad might wear including suits, sweaters, T-shirts, ties, hats, jeans and button-down shirts. You'll also need colored paper, markers, tape, newsprint, a Bible and pencils.

THE MEETING

1. PERFECT DAD

Place the "dad" clothes on a table. Form teams of no more than four. Give each team some colored paper, markers and tape. Say: **Try to create the perfect father. Choose someone in your group to be the superdad model. Use the clothes provided to dress your superdad. Then use the colored paper and markers to list qualities of a superdad. Tape the qualities to your superdad's clothing.**

Have the superdads stand in front while teams describe the characteristics of each one. Then have teenagers each stand behind the dad they'd prefer. Ask: **Why did you choose that dad? Are these superdads realistic? Why or why not? What qualities of that father appeal to you? What turns you off about the fathers you didn't choose?** Have the superdads remain dressed up for the duration of the meeting.

2. LIGHTS! CAMERAS! DADS!

Tape a sheet of newsprint to a wall. Have kids call out names of TV or movie dads. List five or six of these on the newsprint. Form groups of three. Have kids each tell which of the TV or movie dads they think is most realistic and which is most unrealistic. Ask: **How do the TV and movie dads differ from the perfect dads created in the opener? How do they differ from real dads?**

3. THE GOOD FATHER

Form a circle. Say: **In the early days of television and movies, dads were always depicted as stable, strong and likable. But today, some TV shows and movies try to be more realistic. Dads aren't always stable, strong or easy to get along with. Even in Bible times, dads weren't perfect. In 1 Samuel 18–31, King Saul hated David, his son's best friend. So Saul set out to kill David.**

Ask: **What are some common problems you have with your dad? What things are hard to talk to him about? How do you feel when you disagree with your dad?**

Have a volunteer read aloud Exodus 20:12 and Ephesians 6:4. Ask: **According to these passages, what responsibilities do fathers have to their children and vice versa? Does it always work that way? Why or why not?**

4. TALKING IT OUT

Give each teenager a sheet of colored paper and a pencil. They'll also need tape. Have kids each write one problem they have in their relationship with their dad. Then have them each list one thing about their relationship that's good. Have teenagers commit to talking with their dads about their relationships during the next week. Have teenagers fold their papers and tape them shut. Then have them write their names on their papers and place them on the floor.

5. OFF THE PEDESTAL

Form a circle around the papers. Have the superdads from the opener take off their costumes and place them in the center of the circle. Say: **Only one father can claim perfection—God. Earthly dads aren't perfect. When movies, television or our own expectations place our dads on a pedestal—they're bound to fall off sooner or later.**

Hold hands for a circle prayer. Have kids each thank God for one thing they love about their father.

THEME
Forgiveness

SCRIPTURE: Matthew 18:21-35 and Luke 7:36-50

OBJECTIVE: Help kids learn to forgive their parents and themselves.

PREPARATION: For the meeting, you'll need red, heart-shaped pieces of paper, pencils, yarn, newsprint, tape, a red marker, Bibles, scissors, glue and white posterboard.

THE MEETING

1. SINFUL BONDAGE

Give each person a red, heart-shaped piece of paper and a pencil. Ask kids to spend a few minutes reflecting on what they did at home during the last week. Then have them write on their paper hearts every sin they committed related to their families in the last seven days.

Give kids each a 2-foot piece of yarn for every sin on their list. Then form pairs and have them tie their ankles to their partners' with the yarn.

2. LIFE AS USUAL

Assign each pair tasks such as going up and down stairs, carrying chairs or hanging signs from the ceiling. Have them perform their tasks with their ankles tied to their partners. Be sure partners act as "safety nets" for each other so they won't get hurt doing their tasks.

3. "SORRY" ISN'T ENOUGH

Call kids together. Have partners stay tied to each other. Ask: **Was this experience fun? Why or why not? How would you feel if you always had to live with your ankles tied? How is the yarn around your ankles like sin? How does sin tie you down?**

Tape a sheet of newsprint to the wall. Ask: **What does being forgiven mean to you? What's your response to being forgiven when you do something wrong?**

Write kids' responses to both of these questions on the newsprint. Then read aloud Luke 7:36-50.

Ask: **Why did Jesus honor the woman in the story? When have you felt like that woman? When have you felt like Simon the Pharisee?**

FORGIVING YOU, FORGIVING ME

4. TRUE FORGIVENESS

Say: **Forgiveness means healing. When we forgive parents or family members for hurting us, we minister healing to them and to ourselves. And when we're forgiven we're released from the guilt of sin.**

Ask kids to close their eyes and listen as you read aloud Matthew 18:21-35.

Ask: **Think of a time when someone in your family really hurt you. Picture that family member in your mind. How do you feel about that person? Now think of a time you did something wrong in your family—something that hurt your parent or sibling. Do you feel forgiven for what you did? How would you feel if God told you he wouldn't forgive your sin unless you forgave the person who hurt you?**

Have kids open their eyes and write their feelings about the experience on the back of their paper hearts.

5. CUTTING FREE

Have kids each look at the list of sins on their paper heart. Have kids each pray silently about each sin, asking for God's forgiveness and help in changing direction the next time they face a similar temptation. As kids finish praying, use scissors to cut their ankles free from the yarn. As you free each teenager's ankle, look at him or her and say: **You're forgiven.**

6. WHITE HEART

Have kids glue their yarn strips on a large sheet of white posterboard to form a giant heart-shaped outline. Using a red marker, have kids write in the center of the heart, "Forgiven by His Love!"

Close with prayer, thanking God for his patience and forgiveness. Post the white heart in the meeting room as a reminder of God's forgiveness.

60

THEME
Respect

SCRIPTURE: 1 Corinthians 13:11-13; 1 Thessalonians 4:11-12; 1 Timothy 4:12; and Titus 2:7-8

OBJECTIVE: Help kids earn their parents' respect.

PREPARATION: Set up an obstacle course that begins with a tricycle race. The tricycles must be driven carefully around eggs that are set in the middle of the path (like a slalom race). Then have a section of the room where each team has a wastebasket and equal amounts of paper balls strewn over the floor. Finally, place pennies for each team flat on a table next to a piggy bank.

THE MEETING

1. OBSTACLE COURSE

Form teams of two. Explain the rules for the obstacles course: Team members must try to earn respect by first driving responsibly around the track, then picking up their room and finally saving their money by putting it in a piggy bank. Have volunteers time both team's participants. After the first run, reset the course and have the next team members run it. Add three seconds to a team's time any time an egg is hit, a piece of paper is left on the floor or a penny is missed. Add the total times for each team to determine the winner.

2. EARNING RESPECT

Ask: **How did you feel running around trying to "gain respect"? How does it relate to real life? What actions gain respect from adults? What attitudes? If adults you know had created this relay, what actions would they have had you do to gain respect?**

3. WHAT DOESN'T WORK

Form groups of three or four. Ask groups to each create a short skit that demonstrates one or more ways teenagers lose adults' respect. Encourage kids to be outrageous or silly in their skits. Have groups each perform their skit. Ask: **Is it easier to know what adults respect or what they don't respect? Explain. Why is it important to be treated like an adult?**

4. BIBLICAL ADVICE

Have groups read 1 Timothy 4:12. Ask: **What does this verse tell you about gaining respect?**

Have groups read 1 Corinthians 13:11-13. Ask: **What childish things keep you from being respected as an adult? Is it easy to "put away childish things"? Besides gaining respect, why is it important?**

Have groups read 1 Thessalonians 4:11-12 and Titus 2:7-8. Ask: **What advice do these passages give on how to gain respect? Is it realistic? Why or why not?**

5. HOW DO YOU SPELL RESPECT?

Give group members each a 3×5 card and a pencil. Ask them each to write the word "RESPECT" vertically along the left edge of the card. Then ask them each to create an acrostic of things they can do in order to gain the respect of adults. For example, be <u>R</u>esponsible with homework, <u>E</u>xercise caution in spending money, <u>S</u>top staying out too late, and so on. Then ask the teenagers to think about which one (or more) of these qualities they will work on during the next week.

6. PRAYERS FOR RESPECT

Encourage kids to pursue the qualities outlined by the scripture passages. As a closing prayer, have kids silently read their acrostics and pray for God to help them in each area they listed.

THEME
Parents

SCRIPTURE: Matthew 3:16-17 and Ephesians 6:1-3

OBJECTIVE: Help kids know what makes parents proud of them.

PREPARATION: Ask parents to list things their teenagers do that make them proud. Collect the lists and copy each idea onto a separate slip of paper. Then slide the slips into candy bar wrappers. Make sure you have one for each group member. You'll also need wood blocks, newsprint, tape, Bibles and a marker.

THE MEETING

1. PRIDE BEFORE A FALL

Form two teams. Give each team the same number of wood blocks. Make sure you have at least twice as many blocks as kids in each team. Clear a space on the floor for a "building site."

One person from team 1 begins by placing a block in the building site. Then a person from team 2 must stack a block on top of the first one. Alternately, kids on each team try to carefully stack a block on the ever-growing structure. As each person places a block, his or her teammates must say, "Make me proud!" in unison. When someone places a block and the tower falls—that team loses. Play two out of three. Award the winning team a block with the words "A team to be proud of" written or painted on it.

2. WHAT IS PRIDE ALL ABOUT?

Gather back together. Ask: **Is pride good or bad? Explain. What can the winning team feel proud of? How about the losing team? Is winning the top priority in life? Why or why not?**

Ask kids to brainstorm things they're proud of. Write these on a sheet of newsprint. Then ask them to brainstorm things that make their parents proud of them. Write these on another sheet of newsprint.

MAKE YOUR PARENTS PROUD

3. SIMILAR AND DIFFERENT LISTS

Form groups of three. Have the groups compare the two lists. Ask: **How are the two lists similar? different? Is it important to make your parents feel proud of you? Explain. Which items on the parents' list are easy to do? Which are not? Which could kids do more?**

4. REVEALING CANDY CHARADES

Gather together. Give each person a candy bar with the notes in the wrappers. Ask them each to open the wrapper and read the note silently. Explain that these are all examples of what makes their parents proud. Then play Charades. Have group members each act out what's on their paper. Ask: **Did any of the "things that make parents proud" surprise you? Why or why not?**

5. PROUD FATHER

Read aloud Ephesians 6:1-3. Ask: **Does this commandment apply today? Why or why not? How do "honoring your parents" and "making parents proud of you" differ? How are they similar?**

Read aloud Matthew 3:16-17. Ask: **Why was God pleased with Jesus? How did Jesus seek to please God? How can you please your parents in the same way?**

6. DECIDE TO PLEASE

Ask group members to each write one way they can please their parents this week on the back of a candy wrapper. Ask kids to think about making their parents happy every time they see or eat a candy bar. Be sure to follow up on their progress at the next meeting. Close with prayer for parents.

THEME
Growing Up

SCRIPTURE: Luke 2:52 and 2 Timothy 3:14-15

OBJECTIVE: Help kids prepare for life after they leave home.

PREPARATION: Write each of the following sentences on a different 3×5 card: "Pay car insurance six-month premium, $350." "Give at church, any amount." "Buy groceries for the month, $300." "Take spouse out for the evening, $75." "Get car transmission fixed, $450." "Pay mortgage payment, $500." "Pay charge-card bill, $175." "Pay child's dental bill, $375." You'll also need play money, dice, Bibles, newsprint and markers.

THE MEETING

1. SO MUCH TO DO

Have two volunteers—a guy and a girl—leave the room. Explain to the rest of your group that when the two volunteers return, they'll just be starting out on their own as adults. Tell the group to call out instructions about what the two should do. For example, kids might yell: "Get married!" "Get a job!" "Go to college!" "Pay your rent!" "Buy groceries!" "Save money for a house!"

Bring in the two volunteers and let your group bombard them with instructions. Then ask the volunteers: **How did it feel to be bombarded with instructions?**

Say: **These feelings are similar to adults' feelings when they realize all they're expected to do**.

2. RESPONSIBILITY ROAD

Make a circle of eight chairs. Place a 3×5 card face down on each chair. If you have more than eight kids, provide more circles and sets of cards. Form teams of no more than eight.

Tell kids to imagine they're each a married adult with one child. Then give them each $1,000 in play money. Have the players line up behind one chair. Then have the first player roll two dice and move that number of chairs to the right. Have that player read that chair's card aloud and pay you the designated amount. Then have that person go to the back of the line.

Repeat the process with the next players. Whoever runs out of money must drop out of the game. Keep going until all players are eliminated but one.

Then ask: **How is this game like real life as adults? How is it different? How did it feel to see your money dwindle away?**

3. IF ONLY

Say: **To be ready to handle the responsibilities of adulthood, it helps if we prepare as teenagers. The Bible can give us insights for our preparation.**

Form groups of four. Have each group read aloud Luke 2:52 and 2 Timothy 3:14-15. Then have kids imagine they're adults now. Have them tell some things they learned from the Bible or their faith experiences as teenagers that helped prepare them for adulthood.

Then have volunteers write on newsprint the main things these passages suggest that teenagers can do to prepare for life as an adult.

4. COMMITMENT

Form pairs. Have partners each tell one thing this meeting has made them think about. Then encourage them to pray together, each committing to take a specific action to prepare for adulthood.

THEME
Rebellion

SCRIPTURE: Daniel 1; Daniel 3; Daniel 6; and Acts 4:32–5:11

OBJECTIVE: Help kids turn rebellion from a negative into a positive.

PREPARATION: For the meeting, you'll need newsprint, markers, Bibles, 3×5 cards and pencils.

THE MEETING

1. EXPRESS YOURSELF

Display two large sheets of newsprint. On one draw a positive symbol (+); on the other draw a negative symbol (-). Tell kids to stand near the symbol that best expresses how they feel about rebellion. Ask: **Why did you choose that symbol? Why do you see rebellion as positive or negative?**

2. FAMOUS REBELS

Say: **Rebellion can be a positive force.**

Ask kids to name people in history who accomplished something positive through rebellion; for example, St. Francis of Assisi, leaders in the American Revolution or Martin Luther King Jr. List the names on newsprint. Ask: **How have these people impacted society through positive rebellion?**

Say: **People in the Bible also rebelled.**

Form four groups. Assign each group one of these scriptures: Daniel 1; Daniel 3; Daniel 6; or Acts 4:32–5:11. Instruct groups to each create a rap, telling the story and highlighting each person's positive or negative rebellion.

Have groups each perform their rap.

3. REBELLION GUIDELINES

Ask: **From our Bible study raps and the list of famous rebels, how can we define positive rebellion?**

Write kids' definitions on newsprint.

Say: **People can rebel positively against prejudice, a domineering government or unfair laws, and against those who damage the earth.**

Ask: **How can we rebel without hurting our parents? others?**

67

What might be the consequences of rebellion? When can positive rebellion turn negative? What guidelines do we need to follow in order to rebel positively?

List these guidelines on newsprint.

4. REBELLIOUS ACTION

Say: **Let's put these rebellion guidelines into action.**

Ask: **How can we rebel positively against a specific problem in our home or church?**

Discuss several problems kids face at home or in some other arena of life. Have kids brainstorm positive ways of rebelling to bring about change.

Form groups of three. Have groups each tackle one problem each group member faces and work together to establish a plan of action for each person.

5. PERSONAL REBELLION

Distribute 3×5 cards and pencils.

Say: **You can apply these ideas about positive rebellion to your life. Write one negative way you've rebelled against your parents, teachers or others this past week. Don't write your name on the card.**

Collect the cards, mix them up and redistribute them. Be sure everyone has someone else's card. Ask kids to each read aloud the rebellion card they were given. As a group, discuss ways to turn each negative rebellion into something positive. Refer back to the guidelines in activity 3.

Tell kids to each silently pray for the person who wrote the rebellion card they were given. Close with a prayer asking God to turn negative rebellion into positive rebellion.

THEME
Parents

SCRIPTURE: Proverbs 15:33; Matthew 6:1-4; 15:7-9; and Ephesians 6:1-3

OBJECTIVE: Help kids learn how to honor and support their parents.

PREPARATION: For the meeting, you'll need newsprint, construction paper, markers, tape, a blue ribbon award, Bibles, paper, pencils and a camera.

THE MEETING

1. SHOWING RESPECT

Form teams of three. Give each team newsprint, construction paper, markers and tape. Say: **Your task is to decorate one team member with words, symbols and pictures that show how you can give respect to someone. For example, you might draw an ear to represent listening or an open hand to represent openness. Ideas might include loving, caring, being free to disagree or valuing opinions.**

Award a blue ribbon to the team with the most creatively decorated individual.

2. HONOR AND RESPECT

Ask the teams: **Is there any difference between honor and respect? Why or why not? Is it easy to respect your friends? your parents? Why or why not? Look at your decorated team member. How well do you honor your parents in the ways listed?**

3. DEFINING HONOR

Form groups of no more than four. Assign each group one of the following scripture passages: Proverbs 15:33; Matthew 6:1-4; 15:7-9; or Ephesians 6:1-3. Ask groups to each read their passage. Then ask groups to discuss: **What does honor mean in your passage? Who deserves honor? Why?**

4. WHAT IF WE DISAGREE?

Form two groups. Tell one group they will be parents of teenagers.

Tell the other group they will be the teenagers. Have groups line up facing one another.

Ask kids in the parent group to each think of one statement or action parents say or do such as, "I love you," "Clean your room," smoking, doing the laundry, and so on. Ask the first "parent" to tell his or her statement or action. Ask the first "teenager" to step forward if this statement or action makes it easier to respect the parent or take one step backward if it makes it harder. Continue down the line.

Then ask: **Do parents' words and actions make it easier or harder to honor them? Explain. What's the difference between honoring your parents and agreeing with them? What's the difference between honoring and obeying? Can you honor your parents even if you don't like them? Why or why not?**

5. I WILL HONOR

Read aloud Ephesians 6:1-3. Say: **Even though we may not always agree with them, we must honor our parents. Look again at the decorated team members from the opening activity. Think how you might better honor your parents.**

Give each teenager a sheet of paper and a pencil. Ask them to each list ways they can honor their parents. Then ask them to turn their papers over and write a short prayer, asking God to help them honor their parents when it's hard.

6. ABOVE ALL, HONOR GOD

Form a circle. Ask volunteers to read their prayers aloud. Remind teenagers that honoring God is even more important than honoring their parents. Conclude by taking pictures of the decorated people. Display them on a church bulletin board to inform others about the meeting topic.

THEME
Responsibility

SCRIPTURE: Romans 8:1-17
OBJECTIVE: Show teenagers how to balance freedom and responsibility.
PREPARATION: For the meeting, you'll need newsprint, assorted markers, tape, paper, pencils, paper strips and a Bible.

THE MEETING

1. FRIDAY-NIGHT FREEDOM

Form groups of no more than five. Give each group a sheet of newsprint and two different-color markers. Say: **Imagine this is Friday night. Your parents have given you complete freedom to do whatever you want all weekend. In your groups, write your plans for the weekend using one color of marker.**

Have groups post their weekend plans around the room and read them aloud. Then ask: **How would your weekend plans be different if you had to ask your parents' permission?** Have each group use their different-color marker to make changes in their plans.

2. FREEDOM ISN'T FREE?

Ask teenagers to discuss the following questions in their small groups: **Why is there a difference between what you'd like to do and what your parents allow? Is there such a thing as complete freedom? Why or why not? According to your parents, when will you be old enough to do the things you changed on your weekend plans?**

3. FREEDOM AND RESPONSIBILITY

Read aloud Romans 8:1-17. Ask: **What's the freedom Paul talks about? What's our responsibility with that freedom? How are freedom and responsibility related?**

Form two groups—the Freedom Fighters and the Responsibility Rebels. Tape two sheets of newsprint to the wall. Title one "Freedom" and the other "Responsibility." Have the Freedom Fighters take turns writing a freedom on the Freedom newsprint such as staying out late or driving the car to school. Then have the Responsibility Rebels write on the Responsibility newsprint an example of what responsibility each freedom might have attached to it, such as, "Be true to your word on when you'll be back" or "Take care of the car."

4. PLAN FOR FREEDOM

Form pairs. Give each teenager a sheet of paper and a pencil. Ask them each to look at the newsprint lists and weekend schedules on the wall. Have them each list specific areas in their lives where they wish they had more freedom. Then have partners switch papers. Have partners read each other's freedom list, then list areas of responsibility that are related to each freedom. Have partners discuss their papers.

5. NEGOTIATING LIMITS

Say: **Often we feel like our parents keep us in chains. They don't give us any freedom. But sometimes our limited freedom simply reflects our lack of responsibility.**

Ask kids each to talk about their lists of "freedom wants" with their parents. Have them ask their parents what responsibilities they must develop to have those freedoms.

6. UNCHAINED

Form a circle. Go around the circle and "shackle" kids' hands behind their backs using chains made from strips of paper and tape. Say: **Though we may feel bound by certain restrictions at home or school, in Christ we're free. After I read Romans 8:1-4, celebrate your freedom by breaking your chains. Let this seal your commitment to responsibility with your freedom**.

Read aloud Romans 8:1-4 and have teenagers break their chains together.

MY
RELATIONSHIPS

THEME
Hypocrisy

SCRIPTURE: Matthew 23:1-36
OBJECTIVE: Help kids learn to overcome hypocrisy in their lives—and help friends do the same.
PREPARATION: For the meeting, you'll need paper plates, markers, tape and Popsicle sticks. You'll also need newsprint and Bibles.

THE MEETING

1. TWO-FACED OPENER

As kids arrive, give them each two paper plates, markers, tape and Popsicle sticks. Ask them each to create two different masks with these supplies. One mask should represent a Christian attitude. The other mask should represent a non-Christian attitude. Tell teenagers they'll have a chance to display both Christian and non-Christian attitudes during the opening activity.

Have group members mingle while holding the Christian attitude masks in front of their faces. Tell group members to talk to one another using the Christian attitude. Call out topics for them to discuss: drug abuse, sexual immorality, cheating in school, evangelism, and so on.

In the middle of the discussion, tell teenagers to change masks and attitudes and continue their conversation. Alternate from one mask to the other, two or three times during the activity.

2. HOW DID IT FEEL?

Form groups of no more than five. Ask groups to discuss: **How did it feel to change attitudes in the middle of a discussion? How are these masks similar to the masks some Christians wear in real life? Does it bother you when you see hypocrisy like this? Why or why not?**

3. TWO-FACED PLACES

Gather together. Brainstorm situations when Christians are tempted to "put on masks." List ideas on newsprint. Ask: **Are you a hypocrite if you're pressured into doing something you wouldn't normally do? Why or why not? Do all hypocrites willfully try to deceive** those around them? Why or why not? Why do people wear hypocritical masks?

4. BIBLICAL HYPOCRITES

Form the same groups used in activity 2. Have groups read aloud Matthew 23:1-36. Have group members identify the Pharisees' hypocritical actions. Have them list these on the masks used in the opening activity. Ask: **Why was Jesus so upset at the Pharisees? What was Jesus' message to the Pharisees?**

5. MY HYPOCRISIES

Ask group members to take their masks and find a quiet place in the room. Have them take a moment to reflect on times when they've acted like the Pharisees. Ask them to pray silently for strength to be true to God—both inwardly and outwardly.

6. TOGETHER WE CAN

Form a circle. Ask group members to hold both masks in front of their faces. Have group members take turns saying "Lord, help me to be true to you and myself...always" as they take down their masks and throw them into the center of the circle. After the last mask is tossed, close with a group hug.

THEME
Friendship

SCRIPTURE: 1 Samuel 18:1-4; 20:1-16, 42; 23:16-17; Proverbs 11:13; 17:17; 18:24; and John 15:13

OBJECTIVE: Show kids how to develop friendship-building qualities.

PREPARATION: Gather enough deflated balloons for each person to have two. Write the following friendship-building qualities on slips of paper (you'll need one for each person): "fun to be with," "encouraging," "forgiving," "loyal," "listens," "shares personal problems," "honest," "supportive," "trustworthy," "has a sense of humor." Place the traits in separate different-size balloons. Don't blow up the balloons. You'll need one prepared balloon for each person. You'll use the rest of the deflated balloons for activity 6. You'll also need newsprint, lollipops, tape, markers, paper, Bibles and pencils.

THE MEETING

1. BIG BANG

Form a circle and place the deflated balloons in the center. Let kids each select a balloon, blow it up and tie it off. Ask: **How are friendships like these balloons?**

Talk about how friendships come in different sizes, are fun and require careful attention. Have kids each burst their balloon and read aloud the friendship-building quality inside.

2. FRIENDSHIP DEMONSTRATION

Form pairs. Have pairs each create a short skit demonstrating how friendship-building qualities can help a friendship. Have pairs each perform their skit. Ask: **How can you develop these qualities? What are some specific ways you can become a better friend?**

Write kids' ideas on newsprint.

77

BEING THE BEST FRIEND EVER

3. FRIENDSHIP VALUES

Read aloud the following Bible verses: Proverbs 11:13; 17:17; 18:24; and John 15:13.

After you read each verse, ask: **Do you agree or disagree with the ideas in this verse? Explain. What are some friendship-building qualities mentioned in this verse?**

Say: **A great friendship developed between David before he became king and Jonathan, King Saul's son.**

Write these scripture references on newsprint: 1 Samuel 18:1-4; 20:1-16, 42; and 23:16-17. Form four groups. Have groups race to come up with at least five reasons Jonathan and David were friends. Have the winning group present its reasons, then give each of its members a lollipop. Then have the other groups give the reasons they came up with.

Ask: **Which friendship-building qualities from our balloons did David and Jonathan have? What other qualities do you see?**

4. FRIENDSHIP ASSESSMENT

Give kids each a sheet of paper and a pencil. Say: **Write a personal résumé describing your friendship-building qualities, using 25 words or less. Collect the résumés and read each one aloud without saying who wrote it. Let kids guess who each résumé belongs to.**

5. FRIENDSHIP COMMITMENT

Distribute a deflated balloon, a slip of paper and a pencil to each person. Say: **During this meeting we've talked about the qualities of a good friend. Some qualities you have; some you don't. On your slip of paper write one quality you want to develop or strengthen.**

Point out the friendship traits discussed during activities 2 and 3. Have kids each place their slip of paper inside their balloon, inflate the balloon and tie it off. Tell kids to take the balloons home. Say: **When your balloon loses its air, cut it open and read the paper as a reminder of your desire to improve a friendship-building quality**.

Close by having kids each say something positive to at least one person about that person's ability to be a friend.

THEME
Dating

SCRIPTURE: Ruth 3:1-16; Galatians 5:7-10; and 1 Corinthians 13.

OBJECTIVE: Challenge kids to re-evaluate their views on dating.

PREPARATION: For the meeting, you'll need Bibles, pink and blue 3×5 cards, pencils, a box, paper, newsprint and a marker.

THE MEETING

1. CREATE A DATE

Form trios. Read aloud Ruth 3:1-16. Stop after you read, "How did you do, my daughter?" (verse 16). Have trios each plan a "perfect date" for Ruth to report. Kids can include modern-day activities or silly activities such as camel races and a goat barbecue in their reports about how Ruth and Boaz might've spent their evening.

Have trios each report their version of Ruth's date. Then ask: **What is difficult about imagining the "perfect" date? easy? How do you feel when you think about experiencing a "great" date? a real "bummer" date? What things make the difference?**

2. HOT QUESTION

Say: **Let's consider what attracts the opposite sex.**

Distribute three 3×5 cards to each person—pink to girls and blue to guys. Have kids each write the top three things that attract them to the opposite sex—one per card. Have kids drop their cards in a box or bowl. Make sure cards remain anonymous.

Draw the cards out of the box, one at a time, and tally the responses on newsprint. Ask: **What surprises you about how the girls answered? the guys? How do you feel about the answers? Explain.**

3. RED ROVER

Form a guys team and a girls team. Give each team paper and a pencil. Have teams each list 10 questions they'd want answered during a period of dating someone; for example: Is this person a Christian? Does this person like sports? Does this person like movies? Is this person kind to people? Can I contribute to this person's growth?

Have a team recorder write the questions on a sheet of paper. When teams are finished, have them line up against opposite walls and face each other. Start with the girls team and have them call out in unison, "Red Rover, Red Rover, let (*name of guy*) come over." Have that guy step out from his line to the center of the room and answer any question the girls ask him from their list. After he answers, he must run back to join his line. After the question is answered, have the girls run to tag the guy. If he is tagged before reaching the guys' line, he must join the girls' line.

Repeat this process for 10 minutes, alternating girls and guys each time.

4. DATE CHARACTERISTICS

Say: **Dating can be a growth experience for two people, blossoming into something beautiful such as friendship and mutual ministry. Or it can be a bad experience that actually sprouts weeds such as selfishness or guilt.**

Read aloud Galatians 5:7-10. Write two column headings on a sheet of newsprint: "Blossoms" and "Weeds." Ask kids to call out items for each column that could result from a dating relationship. List each item under the appropriate heading on the newsprint. Then ask for a moment of silence as kids consider: **In what ways do you personally contribute (or hope to contribute) to a good dating experience?**

5. SENTENCE PRAYERS

Say: **If you want to be a great date, follow these guidelines from 1 Corinthians 13.**

Read aloud 1 Corinthians 13:4-8a, pausing between each sentence for kids to pray real-life prayers. For example, after "Love is patient," kids may pray, "God, help me be patient when my date is late."

80

THEME
Gossip

SCRIPTURE: Psalm 101:5; Romans 14:10; Ephesians 4:1-6; and James 3:3-5.

OBJECTIVE: Help kids understand how negative gossip can be.

PREPARATION: For the meeting, you'll need cloth "muzzles" and Bibles.

THE MEETING

1. PSST, DID YOU HEAR?

Talk with one or two early-arriving teenagers about your plan for the meeting. Decide on a false rumor that kids would likely believe, such as "I've been offered a job with a different church" or "A youth group member was recently caught cheating on an important test." Don't choose a rumor that might actually hurt anyone. Have the early-arrivers begin spreading the rumor during the opening of the meeting.

2. THAT'S NOT TRUE!

Form groups of no more than four. Have each group go to a separate room or private area and make up one rumor about one of the other groups. Assign each group a specific group to create a rumor about so all are included. Remind kids not to single out individuals, but to make the rumor applicable to the whole group.

Then have the groups return to the room and mill around whispering the rumors to everyone except those the rumor is about. After a couple of minutes, form a circle. Ask: **How do you feel about the rumors you've been spreading about another group? How do you feel about the rumor that's been spread about your group?**

Ask if any group member knows the rumor that's been spread about his or her group. Then have groups each tell the rumor they made up.

3. GOSSIP FOR SALE

Ask: **How much would you pay to hear what other people are saying about you? How would you feel if people were telling lies about you? What is gossip? How are gossip and rumors similar? different? Why are people attracted to gossip?**

4. IDLE TALK

Give kids strips of cloth and have them tie them over their mouths like "muzzles." Say: **Idle talk, slander, gossip and rumors are all**

ways our mouths can get us in trouble.

Read aloud Psalm 101:5; Romans 14:10; Ephesians 4:1-6; and James 3:3-5. While kids still have their muzzles on, ask them to silently answer the following questions: **How do you feel when you hear that someone has started a rumor about you? How do you feel when your friends gossip? How have these verses changed your perspective on gossip?**

Have kids remove their muzzles. Form groups of no more than four. Have groups each discuss how it felt to be muzzled. Ask: **What are some ways we can avoid spreading rumors—besides wearing muzzles?**

5. RUMOR UNMASKED

Confess to the kids about the rumor you "planted" in the group. Ask: **How do you feel now that you know the truth? Looking back, how do you wish you'd responded to this rumor?**

6. WHISPERS AND PRAYERS

Form a circle. Whisper something affirming to the person on your left. Tell him or her to do the same for the next person. When the whispered words of appreciation come back around to you, close the meeting in prayer. Ask God to give group members strength to resist the temptation to gossip.

82

THEME
Giving

SCRIPTURE: Luke 8:26-39; Luke 17:11-19; and John 9:1-25, 34-38

OBJECTIVE: Challenge kids to receive God's gifts graciously while they learn how to give.

PREPARATION: For the meeting, you'll need a nicely wrapped gift box, magazine pictures, paper, pencils, masking tape, 3×5 cards, construction paper, marker, a shabbily wrapped gift, and candy or gum.

THE MEETING

1. GIFT BOX OPENER

Bring a nicely wrapped gift box with a removable top. Inside the box place magazine pictures of desirable and undesirable items.

Open the gift and hold up pictures of the desirable and undesirable items.

For each item, ask: **Would you appreciate getting this item as a gift? Why or why not?**

Ask kids to tell about a time they received a gift they didn't want.

Say: **During this season we talk about giving. But it's also important to learn to receive gifts in a Christlike way.**

2. THANK YOU NOTES

Form three teams. Give each team a Bible.

Assign teams each one of the following scripture references: Luke 8:26-39; Luke 17:11-19; or John 9:1-25, 34-38. Have teams each develop a skit based on its verse that shows the giver's action, the recipient's reaction and others' reactions.

After each skit, ask: **If you could, how would you change the ending?**

Gives teams each a sheet of paper and a pencil.

Say: **Often people write thank you notes to acknowledge a gift or thoughtful action. On your paper, compose a thank you note based on your team's skit.**

Have teams each tell about their thank you note.

Ask: **How do you feel about writing thank you notes?**

3. TICK-TACK-TOE TEASERS

Make a large Tick-Tack-Toe board on the floor with masking tape. In each square place a 3×5 card on which you've written one of the following statements:

"Instead of a thank you note, I can express thanks by ___ _____ (make two of this one)." "If you receive something you don't like, don't_____." "A person who always gives me good gifts is_____." "I like receiving gifts on_____." "When I give a gift it makes me feel good if the person who receives it_____." "The best thing I ever received from someone was_____." "It's better to give than to receive." "When I receive something from someone, I_____."

Form two teams. Give each team five sheets of construction paper and a marker. Have one team mark its construction paper with X's and the other team mark its construction papers with O's.

Begin with the X team. Let that team pick a square, complete the statement and place its mark on the floor. Play until all cards are used or a team wins.

4. A GIVING TIME

Bring a shabbily wrapped gift. Inside, place something nice that's hidden in something unpleasant. For example, hide a dollar bill in a finger of a dirty pair of gloves.

Say: **Often we're given gifts we don't want to accept. Gifts may not appear to be exactly what we want, but they're still gifts. Who would like the gift I'm holding?**

Give away the gift and have the recipient open it.

Ask the recipient: **How did you feel when you first opened the gift? How did you feel when you explored a little further? How does this experience relate to receiving God's love?**

5. GIVE-A-GIFT CLOSING

Give a small gift such as gum or candy to each person.

Say: **This gift is yours to use as you choose. Keep it, share it or give it away.**

Close by thanking God for our greatest gift, Jesus Christ.

84

THEME
Peer Pressure

SCRIPTURE: Daniel 3:1-27; Matthew 26:69-75; and Acts 6:8-15; 7:54-60
OBJECTIVE: Help group members stand up for what they believe.
PREPARATION: For the meeting, you'll need newsprint, markers, Bibles and paper.

THE MEETING

1. ONE WAY, PLEASE

Use chairs to form race-track boundaries in your room. Make it small so kids have a limited area to run in.

Ask for two volunteers. Say: **Your goal is to circle the track twice and reach the starting line first. The two volunteers will race against the rest of the group. You may have to steer around people because the volunteers and the rest of you will be going in opposite directions. The volunteers win if one of them gets to the starting line first. The rest of you win if any group member gets to the starting line first.**

Start the race with the volunteers going one way and the rest of the group going the other. Tell group members that they may create "walls" to slow the volunteers down.

If you have time, let other volunteers try their luck. Then ask: **How did it feel to be "going against the flow" in this race? When have you felt like that in real life? How did it feel to be an "obstacle" in the race? When have you felt like that in real life?**

2. STANDING UP

Say: **It's not easy to stand up for what we believe. Sometimes we may feel like we're going against the flow and feel pressured to turn around and join the crowd.**

Form groups of no more than four. Give groups each a sheet of newsprint and a marker. Have groups brainstorm situations when it's important to stand up for beliefs. For example, "When you're at a party and kids are pressuring you to drink." Then have kids circle the most difficult situations. Ask: **Why isn't it always easy to stand up for what you believe? What can make it easier to stand up for your beliefs?**

3. SWIMMING UPSTREAM

Say: **You're not alone in your struggles to swim upstream. In Bible times, many people faced similar pressures.**

Assign groups each one of the following passages: Daniel 3:1-27; Matthew 26:69-75; or Acts 6:8-15; 7:54-60. It's okay if more than one group has the same passage. Have groups read their passages then discuss what pressures the people were facing and what their responses were.

Have groups tell the whole group about their passage. Then have kids each say which person they're most like and why. Say: **We may be hurt by the way we're treated when we stand up for what we believe. But, as was the case with Shadrach, Meshach and Abednego, sometimes a strong stance helps others see the power of God's love.**

4. PARTNERS

Form pairs. Give pairs each a sheet of paper. Have partners take turns attempting to hold the paper up on its end using only one finger. Ask: **How is this like the way you feel when you're the only one standing up for an issue?**

Then have partners each use one finger, on either side of the paper, to hold it up. Ask: **How does this illustrate help from a friend? With friends' support and God's help, how can we stand up for our beliefs?**

Have teenagers close in prayer while still holding up their papers, thanking God for their partner and his or her ability to stand tall even when things get tough.

THEME
Loneliness

SCRIPTURE: Psalm 145:18; Matthew 6:5-6; 28:20b; and John 6:15

OBJECTIVE: Help teenagers explore positive aspects of being alone.

PREPARATION: Write out the instructions for activity 2, "Reflection Time," and make a photocopy for each teenager. You'll also need pencils, paper and Bibles.

THE MEETING

1. TOGETHER, ALL ALONE

As kids arrive, give them each a "Reflection Time" instruction sheet, pencil, sheet of paper and Bible. Ask them each to follow the instructions for the activity. To do the activity, have kids each find a secluded place in the building—away from everyone. If kids don't have watches, make sure a clock is available in each location.

2. REFLECTION TIME

Instructions for teenagers: "During the next 20 minutes, you'll be spending time alone. Use the instructions on this paper to guide you during this time.

To begin, close your eyes for a moment and imagine that you're completely shut off from everyone. You're alone. During the next few minutes, it's just God and you in this place.

Next, on your paper, list three things you're concerned about in your life. Leave space next to each one. Read Psalm 145:18. Take a moment to pray for insight about the three concerns you've listed. Then next to each item, write one thing you can do to help ease your concern about the issue. Then list one characteristic of God that helps you trust God to deal with each issue.

Next, turn your paper over. Write three things you're thankful for at this moment. Then, next to each item, write one way you can share your thankfulness with someone else. Commit to doing that during the next week.

Read the following scriptures: Matthew 6:5-6; 28:20b; and John 6:15. Write on your paper what each scripture passage says about taking time to be alone. Then write your answers to the following questions:

How do you feel when you're alone? Is it easy to be alone? Why or why not? Why did Jesus spend time alone? What value is there in spending time alone?

Spend the rest of your alone time in silent prayer and reflection."

After 20 minutes, gather the group together in the meeting room. Tell kids not to talk until everyone is gathered together.

3. NEW INSIGHTS

Have teenagers each say one word to describe how they felt during the time alone. Then form pairs. Have partners each share things they learned during the reflection time. Ask them to discuss the value of spending time alone.

Ask: **Is there a difference between loneliness and time alone? Why or why not? How can lonely times be beneficial? What insights did you get while spending time alone with God?**

4. TOGETHER AGAIN

For the next 15 minutes, have teenagers play a favorite game or two, and have refreshments. Ask kids to talk about how important times alone and times together are.

5. GOD IS WITH US

Gather in a circle. Have teenagers each share how different the together time was from the alone time. Then say: **God speaks to us in many ways. In our times with friends, God often speaks to us through fellowship. And in our times alone, God speaks to our hearts.**

Encourage kids to spend their alone times searching to know God and his will. Close with a unison reading of Matthew 28:20b.

THEME
Sexuality

SCRIPTURE: Leviticus 18:22; 20:13; Matthew 18:21-22; John 8:1-11; 13:34-35; Romans 1:26-27; 1 Corinthians 6:9-10; and Galatians 6:1

OBJECTIVE: Help kids see homosexuality from God's point of view.

PREPARATION: For the meeting, you'll need newsprint, markers, Bibles, two footballs and small stones.

THE MEETINGS

1. REACTIONS

Hold up a sheet of newsprint with two same-sex symbols written on it—either ♀ or ♂.

Tell kids this newsprint is a homosexual person. One at a time, have kids say or do to the "homosexual" what they'd actually say or do to people who they suspect are homosexuals—without getting vulgar. Be prepared for any reaction—from cruelty to compassion to indifference.

Ask: **Why did you react to this homosexual the way you did? How did you feel as you watched the different reactions to this person? How did you feel about the homosexual? How do you think God would treat this person?**

Say: **Today we're going to discuss a subject that may be awkward to talk about—homosexuality. Our purpose is to learn what God thinks of homosexuality, and not to make fun of anyone or to make any accusations. So be serious and don't mention any names. Let's take a look at what the Bible says about homosexuality.**

2. AND GOD SAYS

Lay the "homosexual" newsprint on a table at the front of the room. Tear the newsprint in half. Form two teams, and give each team one-half of the newsprint and a marker. Assign these scripture passages to each team as follows. Team 1: Leviticus 18:22; 20:13; Romans 1:26-27; and 1 Corinthians 6:9-10. Team 2: Matthew 18:21-22; John 13:34-35; and Galatians 6:1.

Based on what they find in their scriptures, have teams each write on their sheet of newsprint messages from God to the homosexual. After five minutes, ask: **How does God feel about homosexuals? about homosexual activity?** Teams will have differing answers.

89

3. GONE ASTRAY

Have kids stay in the same teams. Clear a space at least 20 feet long and 5 feet wide. Give each team a folding chair. Have teams place their folding chairs side by side at one end of the room. Then have teams each line up at the other end of the room and face their folding chair.

Give each team a football. Have the people at the front of each line roll the ball toward their team's chair and through its legs. Whenever a ball rolls through either chair's legs, the team that rolled the ball scores a point.

Have team members roll the football in turn for two minutes. Declare a winning team. Then ask: **What was difficult about this activity? Since our footballs didn't work right, should we throw them away? Why or why not? How does God feel when people don't go the way he planned?**

Say: **From the Bible, it's apparent that God is not pleased about homosexual activity. But we need to remember that we all do things God isn't pleased about. And he loves us anyway.**

4. JESUS AND SEXUAL SIN

Say: **Let's take a look at how Jesus confronted sexual sin.**

Have kids tape the homosexual newsprint back together as you read aloud John 8:1-11. Ask: **What was Jesus' response to the Pharisees? What was Jesus' response to the woman? If Jesus came to your school, how do you think he would treat kids involved in homosexual activity?**

5. STONE PRAYER

Give each kid a small stone. Then read aloud Jesus' words from John 8:7. Say: **We need to be careful we're not "throwing stones" at homosexuals, but that we're showing love to them as Jesus would**.

Have kids each silently examine their stone as they consider how they may have been responding wrongly to people they think are homosexuals. Ask kids to pray silently and ask God to guide them in their interaction with those people.

Have kids keep the stones to remind them homosexuals can be forgiven—just as we can.

THEME
Partying

SCRIPTURE: 1 Corinthians 10:31; Philippians 4:8; 1 Thessalonians 5:16; and 2 Timothy 2:22

OBJECTIVE: Invite your kids to party God's way.

PREPARATION: Place the following sheets of paper in a bowl: one blue, three red, enough white for the remainder of your group members. Write the following on separate 3×5 cards: "Party 1—You're a wild party. Everyone who comes to your party must be willing to drink a lot of beer, try whatever drugs are present and score with the opposite sex." "Party 2—You're a boring party. You don't have any games, refreshments, music or people of the opposite sex. The most fun thing you offer is someone demon-strating how to make Bonsai broccoli trees." "Party 3—You're a youth group party. You have contemporary music, great refreshments, girls and guys and even a sermonette from the youth leader. You don't have any games." You'll also need 3×5 cards, pencils and Bibles.

THE MEETING

1. PARTY DOWN

As kids arrive, have them draw a sheet of paper from the bowl. Play rowdy music and give kids each a party hat or party favor. Have kids tell three other kids the answer to this question, "Why do you like to go to parties?"

2. PARTY CONNECTION

Say: **Let's talk about how to be a real party animal. In order to**

91

do that, we're going to play The Party Connection—a game similar to the TV show, The Love Connection.

Give each of the people with a red paper one of the notes you prepared beforehand. Have the three red people sit together on the left side of the room. Sit at the front of the room with the blue person.

Give the audience members each a 3×5 card and a pencil. Then ask the blue person: **What are you looking for in a party? Is it hard to find a good party these days? Why or why not?**

Say: **Let's take a look at our parties.** One at a time, have the parties tell about themselves. Afterward, have the audience members vote for which party the blue person should go to. Ask the blue person: **Which party do you choose?**

Tally the audience votes to see which party they chose. Ask: **Why do kids like to go to parties? What makes a good party? How do you think God feels about parties?**

3. FIX A PARTY

Form three groups around each party. Have groups each read aloud 1 Corinthians 10:31; Philippians 4:8; 1 Thessalonians 5:16; and 2 Timothy 2:22. Have groups each change their party to fit these scriptural principles.

4. PARTY PLANS

As a large group, have kids work together to plan a wild New Year's or some other party, using the biblical principles from activity 3. Close in prayer, thanking God for his approval of celebrations and asking for wisdom to party in godly ways.

THEME
Popularity

SCRIPTURE: Matthew 9:27-31; 12:14-16; 15:29-38; and 27:15-25

OBJECTIVE: Help teenagers learn the ups and downs of popularity.

PREPARATION: For the meeting, you'll need newsprint, markers, tape and Bibles.

THE MEETING

1. MOST POPULAR

As kids arrive, give them each newsprint and markers. Have kids each make self-portrait posters with their names on them. Then say: **Your goal is to become the most popular teenager here. To do that, you must collect the most signatures on your poster. Each person may sign only two posters. Before the poster signing begins, each of you must convince other kids to sign your poster by explaining why you're the best candidate for the "most popular person." Make up things about yourself that'll convince others to vote for you.**

Have kids each take no more than one minute to describe why they should be the "most popular person." Then have kids start signing the posters. After a few minutes, call time.

2. POPULARITY TRAITS

Tape the posters to the wall. Determine the top three winners. Then ask: **What prompted people to sign these posters? What promises or characteristics made these people seem most popular?**

Tape a blank sheet of newsprint to the wall and give kids each a marker. Have kids crowd around the newsprint and each write one or two words that describe both good and bad characteristics of popular people.

Form groups of no more than four. Have the groups discuss: **Which of the characteristics are most appealing? least? What's the best thing about being popular? the worst thing?**

3. JESUS' POPULARITY

Form groups of no more than five. Have groups each read aloud Matthew 9:27-31; 12:14-16; 15:29-38; and 27:15-25.

Have groups each discuss: **Did Jesus want to be popular? Why or why not? What happened to Jesus' popularity in Matthew 27:15-25?**

IS IT COOL TO BE POPULAR?

How is the popularity Jesus had like the popularity people have today? Is popularity good or bad? Explain.

4. GOAL OR CIRCUMSTANCE

Form new groups of no more than four. Have half the groups plan short skits about trying to be popular. Have the other groups plan short skits about not trying to be popular, but being popular anyway. Suggest they use a school setting for the skits. After the skits, ask: **Is it cool to be popular? Why or why not?**

5. COVER OF THE ROLLED STONE

Say: **Musicians and other public figures often think they've "made it" when they get their picture on the cover of Rolling Stone magazine. But this kind of popularity is fleeting. Just as Jesus was at one time popular and later unpopular, so our popularity comes and goes. But Jesus' Resurrection proves that God thinks we're each important regardless of how popular we are.**

Have kids design a wall-size "Rolled Stone" magazine cover using newsprint and markers. Then, in a closing ceremony, have kids each walk up to the magazine cover and tape their self-portrait posters from the opening activity to it. Close with a prayer, thanking God that he sees each person as important and special.

THEME
Sexuality

SCRIPTURE: 1 Thessalonians 4:3-8
OBJECTIVE: Encourage kids not to have sex before marriage.
PREPARATION: For the meeting, you'll need tape, newsprint, markers, Bibles, paper, pencils and 3×5 cards.

THE MEETING

1. KEEP OUT

Choose one guy and one girl. Have kids form a tight circle around the girl. If your group is large, form smaller circles of eight to 10 people, each surrounding a female volunteer. Have the male volunteer stand outside the circle and try to break through to tag the female. Allow the male volunteer several tries before having him switch positions with the girl. Once they've switched, have the girl try to tag the guy.

Ask: **How did it feel to try to reach the guy or girl? How did it feel to be in the center of the circle?**

Say: **Today we're going to talk about how we can stay away from sex before marriage**.

Ask: **How does this game illustrate staying away from sex before marriage? What does the wall of people represent?**

Say: **The wall could represent your strength of will or your decisions to avoid compromising situations. It could represent your friends' help in avoiding tempting times. Let's look more closely at what the Bible says about sex before marriage.**

2. A WORD TO THE WISE

Tape a sheet of newsprint to the wall and write, "A Word to the Wise," at the top of it. Form groups of three. Give each group a Bible, a sheet of paper, a pencil and a marker. Ask groups to read 1 Thessalonians 4:3-8 then rewrite the passage as though they were writing a letter to their school friends. Have groups use their markers to write their paraphrases on the newsprint.

When groups are finished, read each paraphrase aloud. Then ask: **Why should people abstain from sex before marriage? Why does it matter so much to God? What if a person has already had sex— what does this passage say to him or her? How can we help each** other stay sexually pure?

Say: **No matter what your sexual history is, you can start fresh today and choose to keep yourself pure until you're married. And we can help each other by creating a sort of "positive" peer pressure, encouraging each other to stay away from sexual temptation.**

3. ABSTINENCE GRAFFITI WALL

Tape several sheets of newsprint to the wall and write, "Wall of Wisdom," at the top of each. Distribute markers and have kids work together to create graffiti that describe not only why they should abstain from sex before marriage, but also ways they can protect themselves from the temptation to have sex.

When kids are finished, read kids' comments and suggestions and discuss them with the group. Ask questions such as: **Is this a good idea? Why or why not? How will this idea help you abstain from sex? How can you apply this to your life?**

4. I CHOOSE

Give each person a 3×5 card and a pencil. Ask kids to write on their cards, "I choose to say yes to abstinence until I am married," (if they're ready to make this commitment). Then have kids sign their names on their cards and keep them as reminders of their decisions.

Form a large circle and offer a prayer thanking God for his forgiveness when people fail to do his will. Ask for God's help in staying sexually pure and learning to avoid sexual temptation.

THEME
Listening

SCRIPTURE: Proverbs 8:32-34; 22:17-18; and John 5:24

OBJECTIVE: Help teenagers practice listening skills.

PREPARATION: Collect several radios and cassette players. Set them around the room and turn them all on. Crank up the noise level in the room as kids arrive. You'll also need 3×5 cards, pencils, newsprint, markers, tape and Bibles.

THE MEETING

1. HEAR YE, HEAR YE

Have teenagers stand in groups of no more than five. During this activity, you'll have to shout over the noises in the room. Say: **In your groups, you'll have three minutes to talk about times when someone didn't listen to you or when you didn't listen to someone else. You'll all need to talk loudly at the same time. Then when I turn off the music, you must all be silent.**

Have the teenagers begin talking. After three minutes, turn off all the radios and cassette players. When the last one is turned off, the room should become completely silent.

2. LISTENING

Silently distribute a 3×5 card and a pencil to each teenager. Say: **Listen.** *(Pause)* **As you listen to the sounds of the quiet room, write on your 3×5 card what you hear. You'll have two minutes.**

Remind teenagers to remain silent as they listen to the sounds in the room. After two minutes, have teenagers form a circle. Ask: **How did you feel when the room was so noisy? Was it easy or difficult to communicate during that time? Explain. During the silent time, what did you hear?** *(Have kids read from their 3×5 cards)* **In which environment were you a better listener? Explain. What does it take to be a good listener?**

3. HEARING

Form groups of no more than six teenagers. Ask them to discuss the difference between listening and hearing. Then have each group create

LEARNING TO LISTEN

a skit that demonstrates one example of poor listening and one of good listening.

Have groups each present their skits. Then, list on newsprint some do's and don'ts of good listening based on the skits. "Do" examples: do be patient, do empathize, do concentrate. "Don't" examples: don't interrupt, don't volunteer advice, don't assume.

Ask: **Is it easy to be a good listener? Why or why not?**

4. LISTEN CAREFULLY

Write the following scriptures, each on a different sheet of newsprint: Proverbs 8:32-34; 22:17-18; and John 5:24. Tape the newsprint sheets to the wall. Read aloud the scriptures. After each one, have a volunteer write on the appropriate newsprint why it's important to listen to God, based on that scripture. Ask: **How can we listen to God? What are the benefits of being a good listener? What might we miss if we don't listen to God? What might we miss if we don't listen to other people? What can we learn about how to listen from these scriptures?**

5. I HEAR YOU

Form pairs. Have partners take turns describing a concern, joy or dream they have. After each partner shares, have him or her pause for a moment of silence and listen to God. Then form a circle. Close with a time of silent prayer. Then have each teenager say a one- or two-word prayer. Encourage kids to take their 3×5 cards home as reminders to stop and listen to others.

THEME
Enemies

SCRIPTURE: Matthew 5:43-48 and Romans 12:14-21

OBJECTIVE: Challenge your kids to love their enemies the way Jesus loved—unconditionally.

PREPARATION: For the meeting, you'll need slips of paper marked with blue or red markers, a sock, paper, pencils, newsprint, tape, markers, scissors, magazines and Bibles.

THE MEETING

1. TOSS THE SOCK

As you welcome kids to the meeting, give each one a slip of paper marked with either a blue or red marker (prepare equal numbers of both)—tell kids not to reveal the color on their slips of paper. Create an open space in the middle of the room, and place a chair for a goal at either end of the open space. Ask one person with a red slip and one person with a blue slip to each play goalie in front of one of the goals. Have the rest of the kids scatter throughout the open area.

Say: **We're going to play a game called Toss the Sock. I've secretly divided you into two teams—the blue team and the red team** (indicate the blue-team goal and the red-team goal). **You're not allowed to show anyone else your slip of paper, and you're not allowed to move from your spot on the floor. The object of the game is to throw the sock to your teammates, getting the sock close enough to the opposing team's goal to throw it under and through the chair. Team members must each try to guard their goal any way they can. Here's the catch—when you toss the sock to each other, you won't know which team each person belongs to because you don't have to tell the truth when someone asks which team you're on.**

Start the game by rolling up a sock into a ball and throwing it to one of the kids. When three or four goals have been scored, stop. Ask: **How did you feel during the game? Was it hard to trust people? Why or why not? What emotions did you feel toward people you thought were friends but turned out to be enemies?**

2. WHO'S MY ENEMY?

Say: **Gang members often feel the same emotions you just experienced. Gang violence is a real problem in many cities and towns. Hatred for rival "gangbangers" consumes the lives of these teenagers. What would happen if gang members suddenly started loving and serving their enemies instead of attacking them? What would happen if we did the same?**

Give kids each a sheet of paper and a pencil. Ask them to list all their enemies by name—people they don't like and people who don't like them. Tell kids no one else will see their lists. Have kids each put their list in their pocket or purse and keep it until later.

3. SAY WHAT?

Have kids get back into the teams they formed for activity 1. Tape two sheets of newsprint to the wall and give teams each markers, tape, scissors and a small stack of magazines. Have kids on the red team use their supplies to create a mural depicting things people say and do to enemies. Have kids on the blue team use their supplies to create a mural depicting things people say and do to friends. Discuss how the two lists differ and how they are the same.

4. NO MORE ENEMIES

Remove the "enemies mural" created by the red team from the wall and lay it on a table at the front of the room. Ask kids to commit to loving their enemies by joining God's love gang. To join, they should bring their enemy list up to the front, them tear their list into small pieces and drop the pieces on the enemies mural.

5. CHEERS TO YOU

Form two new teams by mixing members of the red and blue teams. Have teams read Matthew 5:43-48 and Romans 12:14-21 and create a cheer that summarizes the scripture's attitude. Have teams cheer for each other. Then join hands in front of the "friends" mural and ask kids to pray that God will give them the strength to love their enemies.

THEME
Marriage

SCRIPTURE: Genesis 2:24; Proverbs 20:6; 31:10-12; Mark 10:9; 1 Corinthians 7:1-3; 2 Corinthians 6:14-18; Hebrews 13:4; and 1 Peter 3:3-4

OBJECTIVE: Help kids decide how to choose a marriage partner.

PREPARATION: Decorate your youth room with wedding decorations such as bells, white crepe paper and flowers. You'll also need newsprint, markers, Bibles, paper, pencils, building blocks, and old or blank wedding invitations.

THE MEETING

1. THE MARRIAGE GAME

Play a version of The Dating Game to get things going. Ask for four volunteers—three girls and a guy (or three guys and a girl). Have the three girls sit on one side of a partition, with the guy on the other side. Give the guy a paper with the following questions on it:

● Bachelorette #___, describe your idea of the perfect date.

● Bachelorette #___, what do you think is the most important characteristic of a good boyfriend-girlfriend relationship?

● Bachelorette #___, what's one thing about you that would make you a wonderful girlfriend (boyfriend)?

● Bachelorette #___, which percentage best describes the perfect marriage relationship: 50-50, 60-40, 99-1 or 100-100? Why?

Have the guy ask each question (add more if you like) of at least two of the three girls. Tell the girls to disguise their voices to make it more fun. After the questions are asked, tell the guy to pick the girl who impresses him most. Then, tell the guy and the audience that the prize he and his "date" will receive is a life together—married!

2. WAIT... SOMETHING'S WRONG!

Ask the guy: **How did you feel during the game? Was it easy to make your decision?**

Ask the group members: **What (if anything) is wrong with the** prize awarded in the game? Based solely on the questions asked and the answers received, does the guy have enough information on which to base a lifelong commitment? Why or why not? What's missing?

3. MARRIAGE PARTNER QUESTIONS

Have group members list on newsprint questions potential marriage partners should know the answers to. For example: What does he or she believe in? What are his or her hobbies? What are his or her worst habits? Then ask: **How many of these questions can be answered right away? How many take time before you can know the answer? Do all the answers have to be exactly what you want before you can marry someone?**

4. SCRIPTURE QUESTIONS

Form groups of three. Give each group a sheet of paper and a pencil. Have each group read the following scripture passages: Genesis 2:24; Proverbs 20:6; 31:10-12; Mark 10:9; 1 Corinthians 7:1-3; 2 Corinthians 6:14-18; Hebrews 13:4; and 1 Peter 3:3-4. Ask groups to each write on a sheet of paper their answer to the question: **What do these scriptures recommend about choosing an appropriate marriage partner?** Have groups tell about their answers.

5. WHEN FOOLS RUSH IN

Form two groups and give each a supply of blocks. Ask one to build a tower that represents a marriage of people who rush into a relationship. Ask the other group to build a tower representing a marriage of people who take time to get to know each other. Ask: **Which structure would hold up better in a storm? How is this true in relationships?**

6. MY MARRIAGE PARTNER PLAN

Give group members each a wedding invitation. Ask them to each choose some of the questions from the newsprint list and scripture passages from the previous sections to write on the invitation. This will be a personal reminder of the important things to consider when choosing a marriage partner. Close with prayer.

THEME
Evangelism

SCRIPTURE: Matthew 9:1-13; Luke 5:27-32; 9:16-17; John 15:12; and 1 Corinthians 10:24

OBJECTIVE: Show kids that evangelism doesn't have to be a negative experience.

PREPARATION: Gather a 3×5 card for each person in your group. On half of the cards write, "You may only say 'Repent and be saved' during the first activity." On the other half of the cards, write personal needs such as, "You need help with your homework, so ask other people for help," "You feel depressed, so ask to talk with someone" and "You're unsure about a relationship with a boyfriend or girlfriend, so ask someone for advice." You'll also need newsprint, Bibles and markers.

THE MEETING

1. HE WHO HAS EARS

As kids arrive, give each a card—alternating the "You may only say" cards and the personal needs cards. Tell kids to follow the instructions on their cards and start talking to someone in the room. After three minutes, form a circle. Ask those with personal needs cards: **Who did you talk to? Why? How did you feel when you asked for help and were told "Repent and be saved," instead? Were you turned off or challenged by the "salvation message" you received from some people? Did they say something wrong? Why or why not?**

Ask those with "You may only say" cards: **How did you feel when someone asked you for help and your response was simply, "Repent and be saved"? Did you successfully share your faith with these people? Why or why not?**

Ask: **How was this activity like sharing your faith in real life?**

2. MEETING NEEDS AND SHARING FAITH

Form partners. Ask pairs to each come up with a one-minute skit on a wrong way to share your faith with another person. Then have pairs each role play that example for the others. After each role-play, ask: **What was wrong with the way this group evangelized? How can you share your faith with others without turning them off?**

3. FRIENDSHIP EVANGELISM

Ask: **When you have problems or needs such as the ones you role played in the opening activity, who do you turn to?**

List kids' answers on the newsprint and record the most popular answer. Read aloud John 15:12 and 1 Corinthians 10:24.

Ask: **According to these scriptures, what should we do for people in need?** Read aloud Matthew 9:1-13; Luke 5:27-32; and 9:16-17. Ask: **How did Jesus meet people's needs? How did he share the good news of God's love with them?**

Form pairs. Ask each pair to discuss: **Is it easier to talk to a friend or a stranger about your relationship with God? Explain. How can helping a person in need give you a chance to share your faith? How would Jesus talk about the good news of God's love to kids at your school?**

4. COMMITMENT

Form pairs. Ask partners to each think of one person they know who's in need. Then ask them to tell each other one way they can reach out to that person during the next week. Challenge partners to support each other in reaching out. Close by asking partners to pray for the person they chose.

THEME
Putdowns

SCRIPTURE: Proverbs 14:17; John 13:34; and Ephesians 4:24-32

OBJECTIVE: Discuss subtle and not-so-subtle ways people hurt each other.

PREPARATION: For the meeting, you'll need scrap paper, newsprint, markers and Bibles.

THE MEETING

1. OUCH!

Give kids each a supply of scrap paper to crumple into balls. Have kids line up at one end of the room and number off. Say: **I'll call out random numbers. When your number is called, run to the other end of the room and back. As you return to your line, you'll have to duck and dodge, because everyone else will try to hit you with the paper balls before you get back. Each time you're hit, say "ouch" loudly.**

Call out random numbers until you've called each person's number at least once.

2. REFLECTING ON PAIN

Have kids help you pick up the paper and place it in a pile to use later. Form a circle. Ask: **How did you feel when your number was called? How is that like your feelings when you walk by a group of people who call out insults or putdowns? How did you feel when you were hit by the paper balls? How is that like your feelings when you're ridiculed or put down?**

3. THE SHAPE OF PUTDOWNS

Say: **Putdowns can take many different shapes. Some are as obvious as being pummeled by paper, but others are more subtle.**

Form groups of no more than four. Have them brainstorm ways people put each other down, such as not including someone in activities and whispering behind another's back. Have groups list their ideas on newsprint. Then ask groups each to share their ideas.

Ask: **Which of these putdowns hurts the most? Why do people put down others?**

4. PICKING UP

Have kids each pick up one crumpled paper. Form trios and give each a marker. Say: **Talk among your trios about ways you can stop people from using the putdowns we listed earlier. Uncrumple the paper balls and write your suggestions on them. Begin by checking out the advice in Proverbs 14:17 and Ephesians 4:24-32.**

After 10 minutes, have groups each read their suggestions.

5. BUILDING UP

Have kids build a cross with their papers, and then form a circle around it. Ask a volunteer to read aloud John 13:34. Say: **The first thing we can do to squash putdowns is to avoid them ourselves. Instead, always build each other up.**

Have kids each say one thing they appreciate about the person on their right. Then pray, asking for God's help to end putdowns.

THEME
Friendship

SCRIPTURE: 1 Samuel 18:1-4; 2 Kings 2:1-14; Proverbs 17:9, 17; 18:24; John 15:13-15; 21:15-22; and 2 Timothy 1:1-8

OBJECTIVE: Help teenagers recognize important friendship qualities.

PREPARATION: For the meeting, you'll need paper, pencils, newsprint, markers, 3×5 cards, scissors, cardboard box, Bibles and white socks.

THE MEETING

1. FRIENDSHIP CHARADES

Form groups of no more than six. Give each group a sheet of paper and a pencil. Ask each group to list four qualities important for friendships. Then ask each group to demonstrate those qualities, one at a time, using only facial expressions and body movements—no words. Have the other groups guess the qualities.

2. CHARACTERISTICS OF A FRIEND

On newsprint, list the qualities from activity 1. Have someone read aloud Proverbs 17:9, 17 and Proverbs 18:24.

Then ask the group to brainstorm other friendship qualities the scriptures spark and add them to the list.

Give each teenager a 3×5 card and a marker. Ask kids each to write the list of qualities on their card and mark an X next to each quality they feel they have and an O next to any they feel they could improve. Then ask: **Based on your marks, what kind of friend are you? What can you improve on?**

3. TRUST AND FRIENDSHIP

Form a tight circle. Ask for a volunteer to step into the middle of the circle. Ask the teenagers forming the circle to stand facing inward with their hands in front and one foot back to give them better leverage. Tell them they are to keep the volunteer from falling. The volunteer's knees must be kept straight during the exercise.

Make sure the volunteer's eyes are closed and arms are folded over his or her chest. Then ask the volunteer to fall toward the circle. Pass

107

WHAT IS A FRIEND?

the volunteer around the circle and then set him or her upright. Give each person a chance to be in the middle of the circle.

4. FRIENDSHIP REFLECTION

Ask: **How did it feel when you fell toward the circle? How did it feel to help catch the person in the middle?** Read aloud John 15:13. Ask: **How is the trust exercise like the passage in John? How important is trust in a friendship?**

5. BETTER FRIENDS

Cut a large, square hole out of a cardboard box. Form groups of no more than five. Give each person a white sock and a marker. Give each group one of the following scriptures to read: 1 Samuel 18:1-4; 2 Kings 2:1-14; John 21:15-22; or 2 Timothy 1:1-8.

Ask groups each to write a short puppet play based on the scriptural friendship they read about. Have kids use the markers to make hand-puppets out of the socks. Then have each group perform its creative work for the rest of the teenagers. Use the cardboard box as a puppet stage.

6. A COMMITMENT TO FRIENDSHIP

Have someone read aloud John 15:13-15. Say: **There is no better example of a friend than Jesus. Let's always strive to be like him in our friendships with others.**

Form a circle and hold hands. Sing "They'll Know We Are Christians" or another familiar song about friendship as your closing prayer.

108

THEME
Guys

SCRIPTURE: Genesis 39:1-23, 1 Samuel 17:20-51; Daniel 6:1-28; Acts 7:1-60; and 1 Timothy 4:7-16

OBJECTIVE: Help kids understand God's perspective on masculinity.

PREPARATION: For the meeting, you'll need Bibles, newsprint, tape and markers.

THE MEETING

1. REAL MAN CONTEST

Form four groups. Assign one of the following famous characters to each group: J.R. Ewing, Batman, Elmer Fudd and Mr. Spock. Have groups each devise a "Real Man of the Year" campaign for their man. Groups must each emphasize what qualities their character has that makes him a real man. Give groups each two minutes to present their campaign.

Then read aloud 1 Timothy 4:7-16. Say: **According to this scripture passage, none of these men has what it takes to be Real Man of the Year in God's eyes. It looks like we'll have to choose four new candidates.**

2. REAL MAN WINNERS

Have kids stay in their same groups. Assign one of the following men and scriptures to each group: Joseph—Genesis 39:1-23; David—1 Samuel 17:20-51; Daniel—Daniel 6:1-28; or Stephen—Acts 7:1-60. Have groups each campaign for their assigned man, just as in activity 1. After all groups complete their two-minute campaign presentations, ask: **What set these men apart from others? Do you know men like these—people you respect and look up to? Explain**.

3. WHAT'S IT TAKE?

Form two teams and give each team a marker. Tape two sheets of newsprint to the wall. Have teams compete by writing on the newsprint the most "real man" qualities they can think of. Have them use the four scripture passages assigned in activity 2 for ideas. After five minutes, call time and determine a winner.

Ask: **How is God's idea of a real man different from society's?**

WHAT MAKES A REAL MAN?

Which character traits does God most value in men? Explain. Which character traits does society most value? Explain. Which character traits do you most value? Explain.

4. MANLY PRAYER

Have the girls in your group form a circle around the guys. Have girls each pick one of the real man characteristics listed on either newsprint and pray for that characteristic to grow in each guy's life.

THEME
Girls

SCRIPTURE: Proverbs 31:10-31; Titus 2:3-5; and 1 Peter 3:3-4

OBJECTIVE: Help kids understand God's perspective on femininity.

PREPARATION: For the meeting, you'll need posterboard, markers, tape, personality and fashion magazines, scissors, newsprint and Bibles.

THE MEETING

1. ROLE MODELS?

As kids come in, form pairs and give each pair an 8 1/2×11 sheet of posterboard, a marker and tape.

Show kids a table piled with popular personality and fashion magazines and scissors. Tell pairs to search the magazines for pictures and descriptions that portray the "perfect woman." Have pairs each create a movie poster for the soon-to-be-released sequel to *Pretty Woman— Perfect Woman.* Kids may use portions from many pictures to create their perfect woman.

After 10 or 15 minutes, have pairs each present their movie poster to the others and explain why their woman represents the perfect woman.

2. MEDIA SEARCH

Tape a sheet of newsprint to a wall. Have kids call out popular female TV characters, then write those names on the newsprint. Have kids vote for the three most popular characters. Tape three more sheets of newsprint to a wall, and write the name of each "top-three" woman on a separate sheet.

Form three groups and assign each one a different top-three woman. Give groups each a marker. Have groups each brainstorm reasons why their assigned woman is popular and write those reasons on their newsprint.

Ask: **Would you want your top-three woman as your mother? Why or why not? as your sister? Why or why not? as your daughter? Why or why not?**

3. GODLY WOMEN

Give kids each a Bible. Ask three volunteers to read aloud Proverbs 31:10-31; Titus 2:3-5; and 1 Peter 3:3-4 while the rest of the kids follow along. Then have the same groups from activity 2 each use these scriptures to evaluate whether the reasons their top-three woman is popular are positive or negative. Have them mark a plus sign or a minus sign next to each reason, based on their evaluation. Have groups each explain their evaluations.

Ask: **How is God's idea of a perfect woman different from the world's idea? What does God most value in women? Explain. What does the world most value in women? Explain. What do you most value in women? Explain.**

4. WOMANLY PRAYER

Have the guys in your group form a circle around the girls. Have guys each pick one of the godly woman characteristics listed in Proverbs 31:10-31 and ask God to develop that quality in each girl.

MY WORLD

THEME
Violence

SCRIPTURE: Isaiah 2:1-4; Matthew 5:9-16, 38-39; and 26:47-52

OBJECTIVE: Give kids a Christian view of violence in the world.

PREPARATION: Divide the room in half by taping a strip of masking tape down the middle of the floor. Decorate one side of the room with violent pictures from the newspaper or from issues of Time and Newsweek. Decorate the other side with colorful star-shape cutouts—each with a cartoon violence word such as "BAM," "POW," "SPLAT" or "OUCH" written on it. Make the two sections drastically different—one depicting real violence, the other cartoon violence. You'll also need several bags of large marshmallows, Bibles, pipe cleaners and masking tape.

THE MEETING

1. MARSHMALLOW WARS

As teenagers arrive, randomly assign them to either side of the room. Say: **Depending on the side you're standing on, you're either on the Cartoon team or the Real People team.**

Give each team a supply of marshmallows. Say: **Your goal is to get your opponents "out" by hitting them with marshmallows. You must stay on your side of the room and must toss the marshmallows underhand. When you're "out" you must stop tossing marshmallows and lie still on the floor. Kids on the Real People team are out when they're hit once by a marshmallow. But kids on the Cartoon team aren't out until they're hit five times each.**

Play the game for a couple of minutes or until one team is completely out. Ask players who are out to stay on the floor.

2. THE BATTLEGROUND

Ask teenagers who are still standing: **Was this a fair fight? Why or why not? How is the media's portrayal of violence different from violence in the real world? How does the violence in the media make you feel? Look around. How would you feel if the marshmallows had been bullets, knives or fists?**

3. NON-VIOLENT RESPONSE

Have everyone stand on one side of the room. Then stand by yourself on the other side of the room. Say: **We're going to play the marshmallow game again, but this time you'll be one team and I'll be the other team by myself. It'll take 10 marshmallows to get me out, but only one to get any of you out.**

On "go," simply stand in place without throwing any marshmallows. When you've been hit 10 times, fall to the ground and pause for a minute.

4. TURN THE OTHER CHEEK

Form groups of no more than five. Ask: **How did you feel when I didn't fight back? Is it always wrong to fight back? Why or why not?**

Say: **The Bible gives us solid advice on how to deal with violence.**

Assign each group one of the following passages: Isaiah 2:1-4; Matthew 5:9-16; 5:38-39; and 26:47-52. Have groups each read their passage aloud and prepare an opinion of how Christians should respond to violence.

5. SWORDS INTO PLOWSHARES

Have kids stay in their groups. Give each group a handful of pipe cleaners and some masking tape. Have them collect pictures from the walls and marshmallows from the floor. Then have each group use these materials to create a sculpture of something that represents peace—for example, a puffy cloud. Have groups each explain their sculpture. Then have teenagers silently pray for peace in their relationships, church, community, country and world.

THEME
Witchcraft

SCRIPTURE: Deuteronomy 18:9-15; Psalm 23; Malachi 3:1-5; Acts 8:9-13; 19:11-20; 2 Timothy 1:7; and Revelation 21:6-8

OBJECTIVE: Help teenagers understand the lure of witchcraft and what the Bible has to say about it.

PREPARATION: Decorate the room with string "cobwebs," old brooms, pictures of witches as depicted in children's stories and pictures of black cats. Begin the meeting in candlelight. For the meeting, you'll need short sticks, newsprint, 3×5 cards, markers, Bibles and a garbage bag.

THE MEETING

1. BEWITCHED

Say: **Bewitched is a TV comedy (now in reruns) in which Samantha, the main character, is a housewife and also a witch. Whenever she or her husband get in a predicament, she simply wiggles her nose and "magically" solves the problem.**

Give each group member a "magic wand" (a short branch or stick). Tell kids that by using the wands, they can magically change things. Explain that all they have to do is tap the wand on the ground three times and whatever they're thinking about will happen.

Ask kids to concentrate on something and then tap their sticks. Afterward, turn on the lights and ask: **How did you feel when you tapped your stick? Did anything happen? Why or why not? Why are people fascinated with magic and witchcraft?**

2. MAGICAL DISCUSSION

Form groups of no more than five. Give each group newsprint and a marker. Ask group members to list things they'd do if they had a real magic wand or magical powers such as Samantha's. Then ask the groups to discuss: **How easy was it to come up with things you'd like to change? If someone offered you a magical potion that** would give you powers such as Samantha's would you be tempted to try it? Why or why not? Where do witches claim their power comes from?

3. WITCH-BUSTERS

Form groups of no more than three. Assign one of the following scripture passages to each group: Deuteronomy 18:9-15; Malachi 3:1-5; Acts 19:11-20; or Revelation 21:6-8. Ask the groups to read the scripture, then discuss the following questions: **Why does the Bible condemn witchcraft? How do the Bible passages apply today? How should Christians respond to witchcraft?**

4. STRENGTH, NOT FEAR

Give kids each a 3×5 card and a marker. Form a circle. Read aloud Acts 8:9-13. Ask: **What does this passage say about the power of the gospel over witchcraft or magic?**

Say: **Unknown things often frighten us. But we don't have to be controlled by that fear.** Read aloud 2 Timothy 1:7. Ask teenagers to each create their own business cards using the cards and markers, and then write the words of 2 Timothy 1:7 on the back. Ask them to read their business cards whenever they're confronted by something they don't understand.

5. TWENTY-THIRD PSALM

Have group members gather all the decorations and place them in a garbage bag on the floor. Then form a circle around the garbage bag and close the meeting with a unison reading of Psalm 23. End with a prayer, asking God for strength to overcome fear of the unknown and the temptation to get involved in witchcraft.

THEME
Evil

SCRIPTURE: Romans 12:17-21
OBJECTIVE: Discuss evil in the world and ways to overcome it.
PREPARATION: For the meeting, you'll need 8 1/2×11 sheets of cardboard, Bibles, tape, newsprint and markers.

THE MEETING

1. EVIL SWAMP OF DEATH

Clear a large area in your meeting room. Across one end of the room, draw an imaginary line and gather kids behind it. Point to the other end of the room and say: **From here to there lurks the dreaded Evil Swamp of Death that kills anyone who touches it in any way. Your task as a group is to cross the Evil Swamp of Death until you're all safely on the other side. To accomplish this amazing feat, you have only three tools—these three Anti-Swamp-of-Death Pads.** *(Hold up three 8 ½×11 sheets of cardboard)* **By stepping on them, you may avoid the swamp's evil venom. But each of you who touches so much as a toe or finger on the vile surface will instantly perish.**

Have kids work together to figure out how to get everyone across the swamp using only the three pads. Don't offer any help unless they really seem stumped. As people "die," have them sit to the side, watch and cheer for the others.

2. POST-SWAMP DEBRIEFING

After everyone, or almost everyone, has successfully traversed the swamp, call kids together and ask: **Did you enjoy this game? Why or why not? What was hard about it? How did you figure out that helping each other cross the swamp was the key to overcoming it? How is that like or unlike the way we should overcome evil in the real world? Explain.**

3. REAL-LIFE SWAMPS

Read aloud Romans 12:17-21 and then ask: **What does the Bible tell us about overcoming evil? How can we overcome evil by doing good?**

Tape a sheet of newsprint to the wall and have kids brainstorm things that are evil in the world, such as murder, tyrannical leaders, materialism, and ignoring world hunger and poverty. After several items have been listed, have kids brainstorm ways they can help overcome each evil item with good. For example, if kids listed murder, they could suggest overcoming this evil by praying for the people involved in the crime. If kids listed ignoring poverty, they could suggest planning a fund-raiser and giving proceeds to a local shelter.

4. "GOOD" AFFIRMATIONS

Have kids form pairs by gathering in a huddle, reaching in with their right hands and grabbing someone else's hand. One at a time, have kids each tell one way their partner helps overcome evil in the world with the good in his or her life.

Close with prayer, thanking God for the power to overcome evil in the world. One pair at a time, have partners say "amen" as they unclasp their hands.

THEME
Dating

SCRIPTURE: Matthew 7:12; Ephesians 5:1-2; 1 Thessalonians 5:11; James 2:8; and 1 John 4:7-21

OBJECTIVE: Help kids find healthy ways to deal with date rape.

PREPARATION: For the meeting you'll need yellow and blue balloons, tape, newsprint, markers and Bibles.

THE MEETING

1. DATE DEFENSE

Form two teams—girls and guys. It's okay if the teams are uneven. Give the girls 10 yellow balloons to blow up, tie off and place in one corner of the room. Give the guys 10 blue balloons to blow up, tie off and place in another corner. Say: **The object of the game is to protect all your balloons from being stolen while attempting to steal as many of the other team's balloons as possible. You have five minutes. The winning team is the one with the most stolen balloons.**

Start the activity. Then, after five minutes, count each team's remaining balloons and declare a winning team. (Leader's note: Because guys are often more physical and aggressive in competition, it's likely they'll win this activity.)

Ask: **How did you feel when the other team stole your balloons? How did you feel when you stopped someone from stealing your balloons?**

2. WHAT IS RAPE?

Say: **Today we're going to talk about date rape—a horrible offense in a dating relationship. Listen to this dictionary definition of rape: "The crime of having sexual intercourse, usually forcibly, with a person who has not consented."**

Ask: **How is our opening activity like or unlike date rape? Explain. On a date, have you ever felt the same emotions you just experienced in this activity? Explain. How do you define date rape?**

Be aware that group members may know of someone—maybe themselves—who's been raped and may have strong emotions tied to this topic. If possible, arrange to have a counselor attend this meeting to talk with kids if necessary.

DATE RAPE

3. DATING BILL OF RIGHTS

Tape a sheet of newsprint to the wall and tell kids they're going to work together to create a Dating Bill of Rights. Form groups of three and give them each a sheet of newsprint and a marker. Have each group brainstorm at least five rights every person should have in a dating relationship, such as the right to be respected or the right to be listened to. Have groups record these rights on their newsprint.

After five or 10 minutes, gather kids back together and ask each group to tape its newsprint to a wall. Have kids vote on the Top 10 Dating Rights using the taped lists. Write each dating right on the first sheet of newsprint you taped to the wall. When the Top 10 list is complete, go back through the rights and have volunteers explain why each right must be non-negotiable or absolute.

4. GOD'S GUIDANCE

Say: **Let's check the scriptures to see ways God wants us to treat each other.** Ask volunteers to read these passages: Matthew 7:12; Ephesians 5:1-3; 1 Thessalonians 5:5-11; James 2:8; and 1 John 4:7-21.

Ask: **How does date rape violate God's standards for how we should treat each other? What would God say to a person who had raped someone on a date?**

5. PREVENTION POSTER

Say: **Let's brainstorm ways to prevent date rape.**

Have kids write ideas on a sheet of newsprint. Ideas could be go out in groups; make sure your date knows you aren't interested in a sexual relationship and that you expect him or her to respect your decision; date in public areas; know your date well; don't go too far physically on a date.

Gather in a circle in front of the poster. Close in prayer, asking for God's presence in kids' lives, for protection against date rape, for help in avoiding potentially dangerous situations and for the ability to love others as Christ loves us.

122

THEME
The End Times

SCRIPTURE: Matthew 24; 1 Thessalonians 4:13–5:11; and 2 Peter 3

OBJECTIVE: Help kids face the future with hope and courage.

PREPARATION: For the meeting, you'll need newsprint, markers, tape, bowls, blindfolds, three types of food and Bibles.

THE MEETING

1. SIGNS OF THE TIMES

Using Matthew 24, have kids make newsprint "signs of the times." For example, signs may say, "Wars and Rumors of War" or "Gospel Preached Throughout the World." Have kids tape these signs to the meeting-room walls.

2. THE UNKNOWN

Place three bowls on a table. Say: **I'm going to fill each bowl with a different food, and I want you to each take a turn choosing which bowl to eat from. The catch is you'll all be blindfolded.**

Blindfold all the kids and have them line up single file. Then secretly take the blindfolds off the first two kids. Give them each a handwritten note. One note should tell the person to pretend to eat, and then have a negative response. The second note should tell the other person to pretend to eat and then have a positive response. Tell these two kids to really ham it up. Fill the bowls each with a different food—cereals are a good choice.

While these kids are reading their notes, say: **We're going to use the first two people in line as guinea pigs. Let's see how well they choose.**

Have these kids each act out their appropriate response one at a time. Then tell the rest of the blindfolded kids they can change their order in line if they want to. Some kids will rush to the end. After they're relined up, have them remove their blindfolds.

Ask: **How did you feel as you heard the first two responses? How difficult was it to determine how to line up to sample the food? How did the first two responses affect where you wanted to be in the line?** *(Point to the signs on the wall)* **How are your feel-**

123

ings about waiting to experience this food similar to your feelings about waiting to experience signs of the end times? How are your feelings different?

Say: **Christians feel differently about the end times. Some people are excited, while other people are afraid. We're going to talk about what Jesus wants our response to be to the end times.**

3. HEART SIGNS

Form two groups. Assign one of the following scripture passages to each group: 1 Thessalonians 4:13—5:11 or 2 Peter 3. After groups each read their passage, have them each make five newsprint signs reflecting what their response to the end times should be. Then have groups tape their signs over the "signs of the times" on the wall.

Say: **We can watch and be aware of the signs of the times. But it's more important for us to keep our eyes on Jesus. Jesus wants us to be hopeful and joyful as we wait for his return.**

4. IMAGINE

Have kids sit on the floor and close their eyes. Tell them to imagine the following story is happening to them. Pause between each question to give kids time to reflect. Read this story: **One day while walking down the street, you see a crowd gathering. You hear the people saying something about "coming from the skies." What do you think about?** *(Pause)* **You inch your way through the crowd where you can see the back of someone who seems almost radiant. He turns around and looks into your eyes. It's Jesus! How do you feel?** *(Pause)* **What does he say to you?** *(Pause)* **Keep your eyes closed and imagine this scene. I'll call time after two minutes.**

After two minutes, have kids tell what they experienced. Then close in prayer, asking God to help kids face the end times with hope and courage.

124

THEME
World
Issues

SCRIPTURE: Genesis 1:28-31 and Psalm 104:24-25, 31

OBJECTIVE: Explore God's perspective on the environment and ways to take care of the earth.

PREPARATION: For the meeting, you'll need sunglasses, Bibles, a dollar bill, paper and pencils.

THE MEETING

1. AIR POLLUTION

Tell kids they'll learn the meeting's topic by playing a game. Have a volunteer leave the room. Form four groups. Assign each group one syllable of the word "en-vi-ron-ment." Have groups each sing their syllable to the tune "Row, Row, Row Your Boat." Group 1 would sing, "En, en, en, en..." Group 2 would sing, "Vi, vi, vi, vi..." and so on.

Have all groups sing at the same time. Then bring in the volunteer. The volunteer has to sort out the sound to discover the meeting's topic. Once he or she guesses, "environment," let kids clap for their environmentally sound song.

Afterward, ask: **When the air was filled with noise, was it easy or difficult to understand the song? Did God intend for singing to produce confusion? Explain. What did God intend for the world to produce when he created it? How have people messed up God's earth?**

Say: **Today we're going to talk about how God wants to use us to restore the earth.**

2. SPELL DOWN

Form a circle. Tell kids their task is to name items that have to do with the environment, such as earth, sea, animals and air. Have one person name an item. Have the person to the right of the first person name another item that starts with the last letter of the previously mentioned one; for example, ai**r**, **r**ai**n**, **n**eedles of an evergreen tree. Continue until everyone has named one item. Then ask kids to tell why they think the items they mentioned are important or unimportant.

ENVIRONMENTALLY SOUND

3. GOD'S PERSPECTIVE ON THE ENVIRONMENT

One at a time, have four kids don the sunglasses, preface their verse with, "This is God's view..." and read one of these verses: Genesis 1:28, 29, 30 or 31.

4. PASS THE BUCK

Say: **God gave us the responsibility to care for his creation. When people make excuses for not doing something, it's called "passing the buck." Let's think for a moment of some excuses people make for not taking care of the earth.**

Toss a wadded dollar bill to someone. Have this person say one excuse people may say when they pass the buck; for example, "I'm too busy." Then have that person toss the buck to someone else who names an excuse; for example, "Things aren't so bad." Continue with as many excuses as kids can name.

5. A RAINSTORM OF A BRAINSTORM

Form four groups. Give each group a sheet of paper and a pencil. Have each group create an "environment" acrostic with each letter representing a way to take care of God's creation. For example, **e**quips nature, **n**ever abandons us, **v**aries weather, and so on.

Have groups each choose someone to read their ideas. Ask for volunteers to get together during the week to combine the lists and create a handout. Ask the pastor for permission to include it as a bulletin insert or have youth group members distribute the handout after church services.

Have kids each tell one thing they could do this next week to take care of the environment. Read Psalm 104:24-25, 31 as a closing prayer.

THEME
Drugs

SCRIPTURE: Matthew 5:8; 21:12-13; 1 Corinthians 5:6-13; and 1 John 2:15-17

OBJECTIVE: Help teenagers explore the best ways to fight the war against drugs.

PREPARATION: For the meeting, you'll need a stack of dimes, Ping-Pong balls, bucket, fine-point markers, empty soft drink cans, tape and paper.

THE MEETING

1. FINED FOR MISTAKES

Form pairs. Have partners stand facing each other. Then give each pair 10 dimes and a Ping-Pong ball.

Say: **These 10 dimes are yours if you follow the rules of the game. In a moment, partners will begin tossing the Ping-Pong ball back and forth. Each time a partner drops the ball, he or she must give back one dime.**

Have partners begin tossing the Ping-Pong ball back and forth. Every few seconds, have them step back one step. Have volunteers help determine which pairs need to pay back dimes. Collect the dimes in a bucket. If a pair loses all its dimes, those partners are out of the game. When most pairs have lost at least two or three dimes, stop the game.

2. FAIR OR UNFAIR?

Ask: **How did you feel when you were penalized each time you or your partner dropped the Ping-Pong ball? Was it fair to fine you for your mistakes? How would the results have been different if you weren't penalized the first five times you dropped the Ping-Pong ball?**

3. JESUS AND DRUGS

Form groups of no more than four. Have each group read aloud Matthew 5:8; 21:12-13; 1 Corinthians 5:6-13; and 1 John 2:15-17. Then give each teenager a Ping-Pong ball and a fine-tip marker. Have teenagers each write words on the Ping-Pong balls that describe how they think Jesus would approach the drug problem. Have them base what they write on the scriptures they read. Then have groups each discuss the words kids wrote.

4. DRUG WAR

Place three or four empty soft drink cans on a table at one end of the room. Tape the word "drugs" on each can. Tape a line on the floor 10 feet from the cans. Have teenagers line up at the other end of the room.

Ask: **From what you read in the scriptures and discussed in your groups, how would you deal with the problem? Is it important to give drug dealers or users a second chance? Why or why not?**

Have teenagers one by one step up to the line 10 feet from the cans and say how they'd fight the problem. Then have them each throw their Ping-Pong ball in an attempt to knock down the "drug" cans. If the cans are still standing after kids each have thrown their Ping-Pong ball, have kids walk up and knock them off the table.

Say: **Beating the drug problem isn't as easy as throwing Ping-Pong balls at cans. But with creative ideas and God's guidance, we can help fight the problem.**

Ask kids to choose one or two suggestions given during the activity to try during the next few weeks.

5. GETTING TOUGH ON DRUGS

Have teenagers stand alone scattered around the room. Then have kids each verbally complete the sentence you introduce. Say: **I can get tough on drugs alone by . . .**

Then have teenagers form a large circle, holding hands. Say: **We can get tough on drugs together by . . .**

While in the circle, ask God to give each teenager the guidance and strength to fight the war against drugs. Have kids take their Ping-Pong balls home as reminders to fight the problem of drug abuse.

THEME
Abortion

SCRIPTURE: Genesis 1:27-28; Deuteronomy 30:19-20; Psalm 139:13-14; Isaiah 49:1, 5; and Jeremiah 1:5

OBJECTIVE: Provide facts and biblical points of view to help kids make up their own minds about abortion.

PREPARATION: Ask an adult volunteer to count every 10 seconds during this meeting. Have him or her count "one" at 10 seconds, "two" at 20 seconds, and so on. Write the statements in activity 1 on construction paper. For the meeting, you'll need 3×5 cards, pencils, markers, newsprint, paper, stamps and envelopes.

THE MEETING

1. JUST THE FACTS

Ask your volunteer to start counting when the first person arrives. Display these statements written on construction paper:

1. Last year, there were 1.5 million known abortions in the United States.

2. An abortion may affect a woman's ability to have more children.

3. Pro-life advocates want to ban abortions.

4. Each state decides if abortions are legal.

5. Of the more than 1 million teenage girls who get pregnant each year, 42 percent decide not to have their babies.

6. Abortions were used for population control in China over 4,000 years ago.

7. Most teenage abortions are done on girls from low-income families.

8. The law requires girls under 18 years old to obtain parental consent for abortions.

9. A girl must have the consent of the baby's father for an abortion.

10. Our denomination believes abortion is (finish the statement).

Give each person a 3×5 card and a pencil. Tell kids to each write on their card whether each statement is true or false. The answers are: (1) T; (2) T; (3) T; (4) F; (5) T; (6) T; (7) F; (8) F; (9) F; (10) T or F, depending on your statement.

2. THE BIBLICAL PERSPECTIVE

Say: **Experts often disagree on what's right or wrong. Let's look at the Bible's point of view.**

Give each group one of the following scriptures: Genesis 1:27-28; Psalm 139:13-14; Isaiah 49:1, 5; or Jeremiah 1:5. Tell groups to each paraphrase their verse into a statement that could be used by pro-life or pro-choice advocates. Have kids share their paraphrases.

Have kids look again at the true or false statements from activity 1. Ask: **Based on the verses you've just read, which statements would you say are true or false?**

3. IT'S THE LAW

Form groups of four. Give each group a sheet of paper and a pencil. Say: **Based on the facts you have and the arguments you've heard, write an abortion law.**

Have groups each read aloud their law. Have other groups evaluate whether each law supports the Bible and the Constitution of the United States.

4. BE COUNTED

Have your adult volunteer explain why he or she has been counting throughout the meeting by saying: **An abortion is performed every 10 seconds in the United States. During the time we've been in this meeting, there have been** *(the number)* **of abortions.**

Ask: **How do you feel about abortion now that you've heard an explanation of the counting? Why?**

Give kids paper, pencils, stamps and envelopes. Write the names and addresses of your congressional representatives on newsprint. Say: **You can make your views on abortion count by writing to our lawmakers.**

Have kids each write a letter expressing their view on abortion. Mail kids' letters in the next week.

Read Deuteronomy 30:19-20 aloud as a closing prayer.

THEME
Homelessness

SCRIPTURE: Psalms 31:21-24 and Matthew 6:25-34

OBJECTIVE: Challenge teenagers to understand and minister to homeless people.

PREPARATION: This meeting is most effective on a cold night. Set up a makeshift tent or other flimsy shelter outside your church or youth room. For the meeting, you'll also need Bibles, flashlights or candles, a loaf of bread, water, tin cups, Petra's *On Fire!* album and a stereo.

THE MEETING

1. ON THE STREETS

As kids arrive, direct them to the outdoor meeting area. Some kids may share the blanket for warmth. Say: **Tonight we're a group of homeless people. This is our home for the night. There are no warm beds, microwave dinners or televisions. Some nights we have a place to sleep, but tonight the street is our home. Look around you. Not far away is a warm, inviting room** (point to the church or youth room). **But we're not welcome there.**

Have teenagers share their initial thoughts about what it's like to be homeless. Then ask them to continue to imagine they're homeless people for the duration of the meeting.

2. CONFIDENCE IN GOD

Sing a favorite song. Then hand out the Bibles and ask kids to share them. Using a flashlight or candle for light, have someone read aloud Psalm 31:24. Ask: **How can we continue to be strong and courageous when we don't even have a warm bed to sleep in? What do we have to hope for?**

Then have someone else read aloud Matthew 6:25-34. Ask: **Is it harder to believe these words of Jesus now that you're homeless? Why or why not? How can we seek God's kingdom first in our situation? Are you more or less anxious about tomorrow now that you're homeless? Explain. How hard is it to keep your faith in these circumstances?**

3. FOOD FOR THOUGHT

Take two or three slices of bread from the loaf and ask teenagers to share them. Offer a short prayer of thanks for the food. Place the rest of the bread in a safe place. Then pour water into a few tin cups and ask kids to share a drink. Offer a brief prayer of thanks for the water. Say: **This is all the food you'll get tonight.**

Ask: **What's going through your mind? What are three ways you can collect enough money to buy milk and bread tomorrow? What's one way we can stay warm tonight?**

4. SINGING PRAISES

Sing a few favorite songs. Then have kids each tell about one time they felt warm and well fed. Read aloud Psalm 31:21-24.

5. HOW HOMELESSNESS FEELS

Tell kids they can stop pretending to be homeless. Ask: **How did you feel when you were homeless? Was it easy to imagine life without a regular home or good food? Why or why not?**

Say: **We knew we'd eventually go back to our warm homes. But homeless people don't have that confidence. What can we do to help?**

Have teenagers brainstorm practical ways to help the homeless people in their community. Make plans to follow through with some of the ideas.

6. SHELTER THE HOMELESS FEW

As a closing prayer, play the song "Homeless Few" from Petra's *On Fire!* album. While the song is playing, have kids pray silently for guidance on how they can help the homeless.

THEME
Sharing
Christ

SCRIPTURE: Matthew 28:18-20; Acts 17:1-7; and 2 Timothy 2:2

OBJECTIVE: Show kids how to impact the people around them with Christ's message.

PREPARATION: For the meeting, you'll need a bag of 12 marbles, a penny, a $10 bill, paper, pencils, Bibles, scissors, markers, books, shoes, tape, newsprint and a basket.

THE MEETING

1. SCATTERED MESSAGE

Read aloud Matthew 28:18-20. Then pull a bag of 12 marbles out of your pocket and "accidentally" spill it. Apologize and ask kids to help you pick up all the marbles. Say: **It's incredible how far 12 little marbles can roll, isn't it?** Then read aloud Acts 17:1-7. Say: **Just as these marbles scattered throughout the room, the message of salvation Jesus' followers spoke about scattered throughout the world. They were only a handful of men and women at the beginning, but they made a huge impact on history.**

2. ONE-STEP STRATEGY

Place a penny on a table at the left side of the room. Place a $10 bill on a table at the right side of the room. Ask kids: **If you had a choice, would you rather receive $10 a day for the next year or start with one penny, doubling it each day until the end of the year? If you like the $10 choice, stand on the right side of the room. If you like the one-penny choice, stand on the left side of the room.**

After kids respond, explain that the $10 choice would give them $3,650, but the one-penny choice would give them over a million dollars in less than a month. That's because small sums can multiply into huge sums quickly. Ask: **When have you said or done something— either good or bad—that had a much bigger effect than you anticipated? What caused your statement or action to spread so quickly to so many people?**

Read aloud 2 Timothy 2:2. Say: **The early followers of Christ didn't have access to the electronic media because, obviously,**

133

there were no electronic media. Still, they spread the gospel around the world because they passed on the message to faithful people, who passed it on to other faithful people, and so on.

3. PASS IT ON

Form four groups. Give each group a sheet of paper, a pencil and one of the following items to "sell": a pair of scissors, a marker, a book or a shoe. Say: **Your group is in charge of getting the word out about an incredible new product, the one I've just given you. Your task is to come up with an action plan to let the world know about your product. There's one rule—you don't have any money to spend on advertising or marketing. Write your plan on your sheet of paper. You have 10 minutes.**

When 10 minutes are up, gather kids together and ask groups to each present their marketing plan. Then tape a sheet of newsprint to a wall, and ask: **How could we use the principles and ideas we've just heard to spread the word about Jesus? Do you think these tactics should be used to spread the message of Christ? Why or why not? What's the best way to go about sharing Christ with others?**

Have kids write their ideas on the sheet of newsprint, then title the newsprint "Go Into All the World."

4. IT'S MY WORLD

Form a circle. Place the marbles from activity 1 in a basket (Add marbles if your group is larger than 12). Pass the basket around the room. Have kids each take a marble and say one thing they can do to change the world. Close with prayer, and have kids each keep their marble as a reminder that they can change the world.

134

THEME
Global
Concerns

SCRIPTURE: Isaiah 51:6; John 16:33; and 1 John 2:15-17

OBJECTIVE: Help kids cope in a world filled with crises and problems.

PREPARATION: Place two floor fans in your meeting room. Buy two posters and cut them into 25- to 30-piece puzzles. Also cut construction paper into similar-size pieces. Keep them separate from the puzzle pieces. For activity 3, cut a cross out of posterboard, then cut the cross into puzzle pieces. You'll need the album or cassette *Celebrate This Heartbeat* by Randy Stonehill. You'll also need Bibles.

THE MEETING

1. OUT OF CONTROL

Form two teams. Give each team a poster puzzle and a supply of construction paper pieces. Turn the fans so each faces a different direction (toward an open space on the floor). Have teams each place their puzzle pieces on the floor about 5 feet in front of their fan.

Say: **The goal of this game is to be the first team to successfully complete your poster puzzle while the fans blow directly at you. You must stay at least 3 feet away from your fan. At any time, you can send someone to drop plain pieces of paper in front of your opponent's fan to confuse their efforts. You may not speak during the activity or use any foreign objects to hold the puzzle pieces down. If neither team can complete the activity within 10 minutes, we'll stop the game and call it a draw. Ready? Go!**

Start the fans and play Randy Stonehill's song "Stop the World" from the *Celebrate This Heartbeat* album.

2. PUTTING THE PIECES TOGETHER

Form a circle. Ask: **How did you feel as you tried to complete the puzzle? What methods or tricks did you use to keep the fan** from blowing the pieces all over? Did the blank pieces of paper confuse you? Why or why not?

3. MY LIFE IN THE BIG BREEZE

Form groups of no more than four. Have each group compare the activity of putting the puzzle together in the wind to what it's like to live life as a Christian in the world. Give each group some of the posterboard pieces from the cross you cut up. Ask: **What are some of the world's "breezes" that are blowing into the lives of Christians; for example, AIDS, homelessness, drugs, the New Age movement, and so on?**

Say: **Write your ideas on the pieces of posterboard.**

After a few minutes, ask: **Is the world really out of control? How do you keep your life together when the world's "breezes" are so strong?**

4. WHO'S GOT CONTROL?

Form partners. Assign one of the following scriptures to each pair: Isaiah 51:6; John 16:33; and 1 John 2:15-17. Ask: **According to your scripture, who's in control of the world? Why is the world in tribulation? What assurance do we have as we face the world's crises? What responsibility do Christians have to stop the world from getting out of control?**

5. WINDS OF CHANGE

Turn the fans so they face the same direction. Turn them on. Have group members lock arms and form a tight wall 3 feet in front of the fans. Have kids place the posterboard pieces from activity 3 on the floor behind the wall. Ask a few group members to put them together in the shape of a cross. Say: **Though it seems the world is out of control, with God's help we can block some of the breezes that blow against us.**

Turn off the fans and close with prayer.

136

THEME
Violent Crime

SCRIPTURE: Daniel 6:7-23; Psalm 91:1-10; Matthew 10:29-31; 1 Corinthians 2:1-5; Galatians 5:25; and 2 Timothy 1:7

OBJECTIVE: Help kids deal with the fear of being the victim of a violent crime.

PREPARATION: Meet at a time different from your normal meeting time, but don't tell your kids about the change. Arrange with parents to have the kids home during the new time. Ask parents to participate in the last part of the meeting. Also, meet at an unfamiliar site. You'll need light-color blindfolds, markers, tape and newsprint. You'll also need a card with 2 Timothy 1:7 printed on it for each group member and each parent of group members.

THE MEETING

1. KIDNAP YOUR KIDS

Drive your church bus or van around to your kids' homes. At each house, "kidnap" the teenager and don't tell him or her where you're going. Don't disguise yourself—taking the kids away without notice will be enough of a shock. After gathering all the kids, head to your meeting place.

2. FEAR OF THE UNKNOWN

Before you arrive at the meeting place, blindfold at least three volunteers. Ask the rest of the group members to help those kids maneuver into the building and the meeting room. While the volunteers remain blindfolded, ask them the following questions: **What can you tell us about our surroundings? What does it feel like to enter a strange place without being able to look around?**

Then ask the whole group: **What was it like to suddenly be taken out of your routine and kidnapped to a strange place? Describe your feelings—uncomfortable? angry? frustrated?**

137

Explain that this meeting will deal with the fear of violent crime. Then remove the volunteers' blindfolds.

3. WHAT CREATES THE FEAR?

Form trios. Give each trio one blindfold and a marker. Ask: **Does the possibility of being kidnapped frighten you? What about being assaulted or shot? Explain.**

Ask groups each to talk about and list on the blindfold reasons teenagers fear being a victim of a kidnapping, shooting or an assault. Then tie the blindfolds together. Hang this string of blindfolds across the meeting room doorway.

4. HEALTHY AND UNHEALTHY FEAR

Gather together. On two sides of the room, tape sheets of newsprint. On one, write "Healthy Fear" and on the other write "Unhealthy Fear." Give kids a few minutes to list fears that can be healthy and unhealthy on the appropriate lists. Then form a circle. Place the two lists in the center of the circle. Ask: **Do you agree with the items on each list? Explain. What are the benefits of fear? the negative results?**

5. DEALING WITH THE FEAR

Form groups of three or more. Read aloud Daniel 6:7-23. Ask groups to discuss: **How did Daniel face his fears? What gave him confidence?**

Read aloud Matthew 10:29-31. Ask groups to discuss: **Why does Jesus say we should not fear? How can we learn to count on the promise of this verse? How can we help each other overcome fears?**

Ask groups to each read Psalm 91:1-10; 1 Corinthians 2:1-5; and Galatians 5:25 for help in answering these questions.

6. RESCUED FROM FEAR

On your signal, have the teenagers' parents "storm" the room—breaking down the blindfolds that are across the door. Ask them to take the kids to a local ice cream shop for a time of celebration. Give each group member and parent a small card with 2 Timothy 1:7 printed on it. Encourage them to read it often—especially when their fears begin to overcome them.

138

THEME
Disabilities

SCRIPTURE: 1 Corinthians 12:12-27 and John 15:12

OBJECTIVE: Help kids understand how to deal with people who have physical or mental impairments.

PREPARATION: You'll need blindfolds, earmuffs, paper, pencils and Bibles. If your group includes kids who are physically or mentally impaired, adjust the meeting to be sensitive to their needs.

THE MEETING

1. ROLE ASSIGNMENT

As kids arrive, assign each one a particular role for the meeting. Have some kids pretend they're blind or deaf. Give them blindfolds or earmuffs. Have other kids pretend they're not able to walk. And have other kids pretend they're mentally impaired. Have the "mentally impaired" kids respond only to simple ideas or commands and choose to be attentive or inattentive during the mini-meeting.

Have some kids be the leaders for the meeting.

2. TV-SHOW BACKGROUND

Open the meeting with a brief prayer. Include time for silent prayer to help kids prepare for the serious meeting topic. Say: **The TV show *Life Goes On* is about a family of a mentally-impaired teenager who's been "mainstreamed" into a regular high school. The show deals with the family life and problems of a person who has Down's syndrome. As the title indicates, life goes on, even for families faced with the challenges of a mentally-impaired member.**

3. GETTING STARTED

Have the assigned teenage leaders spend 10 to 15 minutes planning a mini-meeting that's sensitive to the needs of impaired kids. Ask them to prepare an opening activity, a basic Bible study on accepting others and a closing activity. Tell them to plan on a total of 15 minutes for the mini-meeting. Suggest they adapt familiar activities to use with handicapped kids. Have them read 1 Corinthians 12:12-27 for ideas for the Bible study.

Meanwhile, have the "impaired" kids prepare for their roles. Give kids each a sheet of paper and a pencil, and have them list all the challenges they'll face as impaired youth group members. Remind kids to take the activity seriously.

4. LIFE GOES ON

Have teenage leaders present their opening activity, Bible study and closing. During the mini-meeting, observe how the leaders deal with the challenges they face. Remind kids to stay in their roles.

5. DEBRIEFING TIME

After the mini-meeting closing, have kids drop their roles and form a circle. Ask the teenage leaders: **How do you feel right now? How easy was it for you to prepare for the mini-meeting? Explain. How well did it go? Explain. How did you feel when you tried to communicate with the impaired group members?**

Ask the impaired kids: **How did you feel? Was the meeting a positive experience for you? Why or why not?**

Say: **As the show *Life Goes On* clearly shows, it's not always easy to communicate with people who have physical or mental impairments. But it's important to look past the frustration and love them.**

6. SURROUNDING LOVE

Have kids stand in a circle. Read aloud John 15:12. Have teenagers silently commit to reaching out to people with impairments. Then have them close their eyes, reach into the middle of the circle and grab one another's hands. Have kids say together, "We are one in your Spirit, Lord."

THEME
Being Like Jesus

SCRIPTURE: Matthew 8:18, 23-27; John 4:7-15; and John 8:1-11

OBJECTIVE: Help teenagers understand how each of them can be a superhero for people around them.

PREPARATION: Collect four or five different superhero comic books, such as Batman, Superman, Wonder Woman, The Flash or The Hulk. Collect a supply of old clothes, colorful strips of cloth, old leotards or stockings, safety pins, paper, markers and scissors. On a sheet of newsprint, list the following superhuman characteristics: superspeed, superstrength, X-ray vision, ability to fly, ability to shrink to the size of an ant, invulnerability and elasticity. You'll need paper, markers and scissors. Prepare hero sandwiches to serve at the end of the meeting.

THE MEETING

1. COMIC-BOOK HEROES

As teenagers arrive, give each one a page from a comic book. Distribute even numbers of pages from each comic book. Ask teenagers to form groups by mimicking their comic superhero's abilities, then finding others who are mimicking the same superhero. Kids may not speak or show other kids their comic book page.

2. SUPERHERO UNDER CONSTRUCTION

Have groups each choose one volunteer to be their new superhero. Have groups each dress their superhero using the clothes and other items provided. Have them choose only two attributes from the newsprint list for their superhero. Then have groups each present their superhero to the other groups. Have them tell the hero's name, abilities and how he or she became a superhero.

LOOK! UP IN THE SKY!

3. SOMEONE HELP ME!

Have groups each describe how their superhero would handle the following four situations: A family is trapped in a burning warehouse that's about to collapse; a train is speeding toward a school bus that's stalled on the tracks; a bomb in a crowded subway car is about to explode; a woman is hurting because her husband just left her.

Ask: **How did you feel in the fourth situation? What are the limits of a superhero's power? Which is more difficult for a superhero, saving people's lives or healing emotional wounds? Explain.**

4. JESUS THE SUPERHERO

Have a volunteer in each superhero group read aloud the following scriptures: Matthew 8:18, 23-27; John 4:7-15; and John 8:1-11. Ask: **How is Jesus a superhero in these passages? What are Jesus' special attributes? How is Jesus' love for others like a superhero's strength? Was Jesus invulnerable? Why or why not? What are abilities we can use to help others?**

5. MY SUPERHERO ABILITIES

Give each teenager a sheet of paper, a marker and scissors. Have kids each create a superhero emblem.

Form pairs. Have partners discuss the abilities they have that can help others in need. Have partners each write on their emblems two or three of these abilities. Then have partners take turns praying for each other, asking God to strengthen their gifts for doing God's will. Serve "hero sandwiches" after the meeting.

THEME
Grades

SCRIPTURE: Matthew 5:41; 25:14-30; 1 Corinthians 12:27-31; and 1 Peter 4:11

OBJECTIVE: Help your kids gain perspective on grades and success in school.

PREPARATION: Get copies of textbooks, such as math, science and English, your kids are using in school. Create a 20-question multiple-choice quiz using questions from the textbooks. Set up a volleyball net in an open area. You'll also need paper, pencils, newsprint, markers, Bibles and a volleyball.

THE MEETING

1. POP QUIZ

When kids arrive, say: **Beginning today we'll be testing you regularly on your general knowledge. We'll also be sending quarterly grade reports from these tests to your parents**.

Hand out paper and pencils, read aloud the test questions and ask kids to record their answers. Collect kids' answer sheets and ask: **How did you feel when I gave you a quiz you weren't prepared for?**

2. TO-TRY-OR-NOT-TO-TRY VOLLEYBALL

Tell kids they'll play a short volleyball game while you grade the tests. Form two teams. Explain that the winning team members will all receive automatic A's on their tests. Pull aside one or two members of each team and tell them to play the game poorly—as if they don't want to play. If possible, talk with your "poor players" before the meeting begins. During the game, grade the quizzes.

3. WHAT WENT WRONG?

After the game, form a circle. Hand back the graded quizzes and ask who won the volleyball game. Tell all those on the winning team to give themselves an automatic A. Then tell kids about the "poor player plants" on each team. Ask: **How did you feel when your "poor players" missed the ball? How do you feel when you see someone**

143

stop trying to succeed in life? How was the volleyball game like what happens to some kids in school? Is your best enough? Why or why not?

4. BETTER THAN BEST?

Tell kids you gave them pop quizzes to see how they'd react, and you won't be sending grade reports home to their parents. Form groups of three or more. Ask groups to each discuss the following questions: **What grades do your parents expect you to achieve? Explain. If you try your best and don't meet their expectations, how do they feel? Is it possible to do better than your best? Why or why not?**

5. REALISTIC EXPECTATIONS

Give each group a sheet of newsprint, a marker and one of the following passages: Matthew 5:41; 25:14-30; 1 Corinthians 12:27-31; or 1 Peter 4:11. Ask each group to read its passage and summarize how it applies to "doing your best" in 10 words or less; then write the summary on newsprint. For example, for Matthew 5:41 a group might write, "Give more than is asked of you."

Gather everyone together and ask a representative from each group to talk about the group's summary. Ask: **What makes doing your best hard sometimes? According to these scriptures, is doing your best enough? Why or why not?**

6. FLYING HIGH

Ask group members each to fold their quiz answer sheets into a paper airplane. Then have kids stand side by side, shout, "My best is enough!" and throw their paper airplanes in the air.

THEME
Media

SCRIPTURE: Romans 12:2; Ephesians 2:1-10; and Philippians 4:8

OBJECTIVE: Help kids evaluate media.

PREPARATION: For the meeting, you'll need a radio, newsprint, markers, tapes, a few balls of yarn, Bibles, paper and pencils, and coffee filters.

THE MEETING

1. MUSIC MANIA

Form teams of no more than five. Have kids sit on the floor in their teams. Say: **Each team's goal is to guess the songs on the radio before the other teams do. The first team to have all its members stand up and hold hands gets to guess the name of the song. Group consensus will determine whether you're right.**

Turn on the radio and begin changing the station slowly, pausing at each station for several seconds. When kids stand up, stop moving the tuner and have the first team that stands and holds hands guess the song. The rest of the group must then vote on whether the team guessed correctly. Teams get 5 points for each correct guess and lose two for each wrong one.

Afterward, ask: **How easy was it to guess the songs? What are the messages of the songs you guessed? How important is music in your life?**

2. LOOKING AT TELEVISION

Say: **If you haven't guessed by now, our meeting's theme is media—music, television and movies. We've just talked about music; now let's take a look at television.**

Tape sheets of newsprint on the wall. Have kids take turns drawing pictures representing popular TV shows until someone guesses the shows. The person drawing may not speak or write words. After kids have each had a chance to draw, ask: **How easy was it to guess the shows? What are the messages of the shows you guessed? How important is television in your lives?**

3. SORT IT OUT

Form a circle. Give some kids each a ball of yarn. Say: **Beginning**

145

with the people holding the balls of yarn, call out a name of a TV show, song or movie, then toss the yarn to someone else, while holding the end. Keep things moving until I say "stop." The yarn can go over and under and around the people in the circle.

Allow this activity to go on until the yarn is quite tangled in the center of the circle.

Ask kids to step back and pull the yarn taut. Ask: **How is this tangled mess of yarn all around us like media influences in our lives? How easy would it be to untangle this mess of yarn? How is that like trying to untangle the mixed messages of songs, movies and TV shows?**

Have kids drop the yarn and step back. Say: **Sometimes we have to step back from the media influences around us and evaluate what they're really saying.**

4. EVALUATION TOOLS

Form groups of no more than five. Assign groups one of the following categories: movies, music or television. Have kids read these scriptures: Romans 12:2; Ephesians 2:1-10; and Philippians 4:8. And then have them evaluate one recent movie, song or TV show (depending on their category) using the scriptures as guidelines. Then have groups report their discoveries to the rest of the teenagers.

Ask: **Do all the songs, movies and TV shows mentioned seem acceptable based on these passages? Why or why not? What guidelines should we use when choosing what to watch or listen to? For example, "Is it true, honorable and perfect?"**

Have kids brainstorm filters to use when choosing what to watch or listen to. For example, "If Jesus were sitting next to you, would you be watching that movie?"

5. MEDIA MASTERS

Give each student a coffee filter. Say: **Use these coffee filters to remind you to make good decisions about movies, music and television.**

Close with a prayer asking God to help us master the media.

THEME
Missions

SCRIPTURE: Matthew 9:35-38 and 28:16-20

OBJECTIVE: Help teenagers develop enthusiasm for missions around the world.

PREPARATION: Borrow a set of encyclopedias and place them in the meeting room. Purchase two large world maps that show country names and borders. Have volunteers cut out countries from one map and place them in a basket. You'll need equal numbers of countries from each continent—one country for each participant. Hang the other map on a wall for use during the meeting. You'll also need an "international" prize, newsprint, marker, Bibles, paper and pencils.

THE MEETING

1. MAPPING MADNESS

As kids enter, have them each pick a country from the basket. Have kids form groups according to which continent their countries are on—Africa, Asia, Australia, Europe, North America or South America.

Have each continent group design a five-question quiz for the other continent groups based on information about its countries. An example might be: What country invented sauerkraut? Encourage groups to use the encyclopedias to help come up with interesting questions. When groups are ready, have them each ask a question in turn. Other groups may use the encyclopedias to find the answers, but they have only 30 seconds to respond. The first group to respond correctly wins 1 million points. Give the winning group an international prize—such as Swiss chocolate or Mexican nachos.

Ask: **If you could be a missionary anywhere in the world, where would you go?**

Have kids each point to a country on the map where they'd go, and explain why they'd go there. Ask: **What would you do there? Do** you think God "calls" everyone to be a missionary? Why or why not? What reasons do you have for not being a missionary?

2. MY MISSION

Form two groups. Assign each group one Bible passage: Matthew 9:35-38 or Matthew 28:16-20. Have groups each read their passage and discuss how it applies to them. Give groups each a sheet of newsprint and a marker and have them write reasons to be witnesses for Christ based on their Bible passage. When groups are finished, have them each talk about what they wrote.

Ask: **Why don't more people commit themselves to missions? Is it possible to be committed to missions, yet remain where you are? Why or why not?**

3. MAP MYSELF

Gather together and give kids each a sheet of paper and a pencil. Say: **On your paper, draw a map of your personality. Include the good things and the bad, and goals and priorities in your life right now. Be creative and really try to describe yourself with your map.**

When kids are finished, have them explain their maps.

4. NEW DIRECTIONS

Say: **Look again at your personality map. Draw in where missions might fit your personality. For example, does it fit in the part of your map called "fears"? Or does it fit in the part of your map called "priorities"? Draw it in now.**

When kids finish, have them each explain where they placed missions on their map and why. Ask: **Where would you like missions to be on your map? What role would you like missions to play in your life?**

After kids respond, pray together, asking God to build new roads and directions for missions in kids' hearts.

THEME
Money

SCRIPTURE: Proverbs 11:28; Matthew 5:3-16; 19:16-26; Acts 8:14-24; and James 5:1-6

OBJECTIVE: Help kids understand why money can't buy happiness or peace.

PREPARATION: Decorate your meeting place with play money. Tape the money under chairs, behind pictures and on the ceiling, floor and walls. The money should cover the room. Buy or bake a cake with a happy face on the top. You'll also need markers, tape, finger paints, posterboard, Bibles and pencils.

THE MEETING

1. RUN FOR THE MONEY

After the kids arrive, point out the money scattered around the room and the cake. Then say: **The goal of this game is to collect as much money as possible—whoever collects the most can "buy" this cake with his or her money. You can steal money from others, but torn bills will not be counted.**

Say "go." After two minutes, shout "stop" and have kids sit down to count their money. Declare a winner, take his or her money and hand over the cake. If there's a tie, have the winners share the prize.

2. HAVE YOUR CAKE AND EAT IT TOO?

Form a circle and ask the winner: **How did you feel when you won? Did it make you happy? Why or why not?** Ask everyone: **How did you feel when you were scrambling to horde the money? How did you feel when someone tried to take your money? Were you disappointed you didn't win? Why or why not? How is this game similar to our society? different from our society? What rewards do the rich enjoy? What rewards do the poor enjoy? Can money buy happiness? Why or why not?**

MONEY: THE KEY TO HAPPINESS?

3. CAN BUY ME

Form groups of three. Give each group some play money and markers. Tell half of the groups to brainstorm things money can buy and list them on separate play-money bills. Tell the other half of the groups to list things that money can't buy on their play money. Have kids tape the bills listing things money can buy on one wall, and the bills listing things money can't buy on another wall.

Have kids read the bills on each wall. Then ask: **What things on either wall can be taken away from you? What things can't be taken from you?**

4. MONEY FOR NOTHING

Form groups of three or more. Give each group some finger paint, a piece of posterboard and one of the following scripture passages: Proverbs 11:28; Matthew 19:16-26; Acts 8:14-24; and James 5:1-6. Ask groups to each read their passage.

Say: **Imagine your group is an advertising company and you're planning to design and distribute a poster that illustrates the message found in your scripture passage. Together, create that poster with the materials you've been given.**

Form a circle and ask a representative from each group to display and explain the group's poster. Ask: **Do you ever feel like the rich people these passages talk about? Is your poster's message valid for today? What's the difference between the world's riches and God's riches?**

Read aloud Matthew 5:3-16. Ask: **According to Jesus, what should bring happiness?**

5. THE PURSUIT OF HAPPINESS

Give group members each a pencil and a play-money bill. Again, read aloud Matthew 5:3-16. Ask kids to each choose one beatitude and write a paraphrase of it on their bill. Have kids read aloud their paraphrases for a closing prayer. Ask kids to keep their bills with them during the next week as a prayer reminder.

150

THEME
Pornography

SCRIPTURE: Psalm 24:3-5; Matthew 5:27-28; and Romans 12:2

OBJECTIVE: Help kids learn a Christian response to the problem of pornography.

PREPARATION: On a wall in your meeting room, tape newspaper ads for current movies, classified ads for sex-related "hotlines" and magazine ads with "alluring" messages.

For the meeting, you'll need a water balloon, newsprint, markers, tape, major newspapers, paper, Bibles, pencils and a trash can.

THE MEETING

1. SHADOWY SECRETS

Form a circle. Have a volunteer stand in the center. Give one person in the circle a water balloon. Tell kids the object of the game is to pass the balloon around the circle without the person in the middle seeing where it is. Have kids keep their hands behind them and pretend to pass the water balloon even when they don't have it. After about a minute, stop the action and have the person in the middle guess who has the balloon. If he or she is right, have another volunteer stand in the center and play again.

2. HIDDEN ADDICTIONS

Ask: **How did you feel as you tried to keep the balloon hidden? How did you feel when the person in the middle spied the balloon? What kinds of things do people keep hidden from each other in real life? How is keeping the balloon hidden like hiding a curiosity or addiction for pornography from friends or parents? What eventually happens when we try to hide things such as an interest in pornography?**

3. SEX, LIES AND MEDIA

Have kids brainstorm definitions for the word "pornography." Write the definitions on newsprint and tape the newsprint to the wall near the ads.

Form groups of no more than four. Give each group a major newspaper, sheet of paper and some markers. Have groups each look through their newspaper and discuss what they think is pornographic. Have them use markers to circle the pornographic items. On the paper, have them list things not depicted in the newspaper they think are pornographic.

Ask: **What's the common denominator among all pornography? How does our society respond to pornography? What's the difference between normal sexual desires and the desires that lead to involvement with pornography?**

4. GOOD AND BAD STUFF

Have volunteers read aloud Psalm 24:3-5; Matthew 5:27-28; and Romans 12:2.

Ask: **What do these scriptures say about pornography? What does it mean to have a pure heart? Is pornography always bad? Why or why not?**

Form groups of no more than five. Give each group a sheet of paper and a pencil. Have each group create a four-line poem describing the Bible's response to the issue of pornography. Have groups each read their poem aloud.

5. PURE PRAYER

Have each person take down one of the ads from the wall and crumple it into a ball. Form a circle around a trash can. Have kids each take a turn making a silent commitment to avoid pornography, then toss their crumpled-up ad into the trash can. After kids have each made a commitment, close in prayer, asking God to purify the heart of each group member.

THEME
Competition

SCRIPTURE: Joshua 1:7-9; Proverbs 4:10-13; 1 Corinthians 9:24-25; Philippians 3:13-14; 2 Timothy 2:15; and 4:7-8

OBJECTIVE: Help teenagers understand the good and bad aspects of competition.

PREPARATION: Plan to have the meeting in a gym or recreation room. Make four sets of different-color headbands by cutting strips from four colors of cloth. Prepare equal numbers of each color. Then set up four cones or markers at one end of the room and a starting line at the other. Collect a variety of fun-but-healthy food items such as chewy granola bars or apples to use as prizes. You'll also need brooms, tennis balls, newsprint, markers, Bibles, tape and pencils.

THE MEETING

1. RUN FOR THE PRIZE

As kids arrive, give each one a headband. Distribute the colors evenly. Have teenagers put the headbands on and form teams based on the headband colors. Have teams each line up on the starting line across from one of the markers. Give each team a broom and a tennis ball.

Tell kids that each team member must sweep the tennis ball across the floor, around the team's marker and back in a relay race. Explain that the first team to have all its members complete the task will win prizes. Tell team members they may not use their hands or feet to move the tennis ball. Start the relay. When it's finished, have each team sit in a separate area. Award prizes to the winning team.

2. WHAT'S YOUR MOTIVATION?

Ask: **How did you feel when you won or lost the game? Why**

did you want to win the game? Do you agree or disagree with the statement, "Winning isn't everything, it's the only thing"?

3. CHRISTIANS AND COMPETITION

Place four Bibles at one end of the room. Have teams line up at the other end of the room, across from the Bibles. After you announce a scripture reference, a member of each team should run up to the Bible and find the passage. Have the first person to find the passage read it aloud; the others may stop looking. Award prizes to the fastest overall team. The scriptures are: Joshua 1:7-9; Proverbs 4:10-13; 1 Corinthians 9:24-25; Philippians 3:13-14; 2 Timothy 2:15; and 4:7-8.

After the race, form a circle. Tape a sheet of newsprint to the wall and list the team colors on it. Have teenagers remind you which team won each race and place a star next to the appropriate color for each victory. Ask: **How does this chart make you feel? Does it reflect your abilities? What does it say about the teams?**

Draw a column and title it "Effort." Ask: **How many stars should each team get in this column? What is more important, winning the competition or giving your best? Explain. What do the Bible passages say about competition? Should we compete? Why or why not? For what prize?**

4. FINAL STANDINGS

Say: **According to 1 Corinthians 9:24-26, we're striving for a prize that lies ahead. But unlike the prizes and rewards of this earth, our prize will be imperishable.**

Have teenagers each tear off a strip of the newsprint chart. Give them each a pencil and ask them to write a short note of commitment to do their best in all things and not be concerned about the prizes of this world.

THEME INDEX

Practical Resources for Your Youth Ministry

Last Impressions: Unforgettable Closings for Youth Meetings

Here's a collection of over 170 of Group's best-ever low-prep (or no-prep!) meeting closings...and each is tied to a thought-provoking Bible passage! With **Last Impressions** you'll be ready with thoughtful... affirming...issue-oriented...high-energy...prayerful...and servanthood closings—on a moment's notice!
1-55945-629-9

Ready-to-Use Letters for Youth Ministry

110 Easy-to-Personalize Letters for Practically Anything
Tom Tozer
These 110 already-written letters cover practically any situation that arises in youth ministry. And the included IBM-compatible computer disk makes adapting these letters quick and easy. You'll save hours of administrative time with this handy resource!
1-55945-692-2

See Your Kids Explore...Learn...and Live God's Word

With 4-Week Studies for Junior and Senior High Students!

Active Bible Curriculum has become the curriculum of choice in churches everywhere! More than 900,000 books are in use! You have many topics to choose from—for junior high/middle school and senior high. Each topic is covered in just four weeks of lessons...so every month your teenagers will tackle a new issue. They'll learn the Bible and how to apply it to their lives...and they'll enjoy learning! Plus, your church will save money—each book includes a complete teachers guide, handout masters you can photocopy, publicity helps, and bonus ideas—all for one low price!

FOR JUNIOR HIGH/MIDDLE SCHOOL:

Accepting Others: Beyond Barriers & Stereotypes
ISBN 1-55945-126-2

Advice to Young Christians: Exploring Paul's Letters
ISBN 1-55945-146-7

Applying the Bible to Life, ISBN 1-55945-116-5

Becoming Responsible, ISBN 1-55945-109-2

Bible Heroes: Joseph, Esther, Mary & Peter
ISBN 1-55945-137-8

Boosting Self-Esteem, ISBN 1-55945-100-9

Building Better Friendships, ISBN 1-55945-138-6

Can Christians Have Fun?, ISBN 1-55945-134-3

Christmas: A Fresh Look, ISBN 1-55945-124-6

Doing Your Best, ISBN 1-55945-142-4

Guys & Girls: Understanding Each Other
ISBN 1-55945-110-6

Handling Conflict, ISBN 1-55945-125-4

Heaven & Hell, ISBN 1-55945-131-9

Is God Unfair?, ISBN 1-55945-108-4

Making Parents Proud, ISBN 1-55945-107-6

The Miracle of Easter, ISBN 1-55945-143-2

Miracles!, ISBN 1-55945-117-3

Peer Pressure, ISBN 1-55945-103-3

Prayer, ISBN 1-55945-104-1

Sermon on the Mount, ISBN 1-55945-129-7

Telling Your Friends About Christ, ISBN 1-55945-114-9

The Ten Commandments, ISBN 1-55945-127-0

Today's Media: Choosing Wisely, ISBN 1-55945-144-0

Today's Music: Good or Bad?, ISBN 1-55945-101-7

What Is God's Purpose for Me?, ISBN 1-55945-132-7

What's a Christian?, ISBN 1-55945-105-X

FOR SENIOR HIGH:

1 & 2 Corinthians: Christian Discipleship
ISBN 1-55945-230-7

Angels, Demons, Miracles & Prayer,
ISBN 1-55945-235-8

Christians in a Non-Christian World
ISBN 1-55945-224-2

Communicating With Friends, ISBN 1-55945-228-5

Dating Decisions, ISBN 1-55945-215-3

Dealing With Life's Pressures, ISBN 1-55945-232-3

Exploring Ethical Issues, ISBN 1-55945-225-0

Faith for Tough Times, ISBN 1-55945-216-1

Getting Along With Parents, ISBN 1-55945-202-1

Getting Along With Your Family
ISBN 1-55945-233-1

The Gospel of John: Jesus' Teachings
ISBN 1-55945-208-0

Hazardous to Your Health: AIDS, Steroids & Eating Disorders, ISBN 1-55945-200-5

Is Marriage in Your Future?, ISBN 1-55945-203-X

The Joy of Serving, ISBN 1-55945-210-2

Knowing God's Will, ISBN 1-55945-205-6

Making Good Decisions, ISBN 1-55945-209-9

Movies, Music, TV & Me, ISBN 1-55945-213-7

Psalms, ISBN 1-55945-234-X

Real People, Real Faith, ISBN 1-55945-238-2

Revelation, ISBN 1-55945-229-3

School Struggles, ISBN 1-55945-201-3

Sex: A Christian Perspective, ISBN 1-55945-206-4

Who Is God?, ISBN 1-55945-218-8

Who Is Jesus?, ISBN 1-55945-219-6

Who Is the Holy Spirit?, ISBN 1-55945-217-X

Your Life as a Disciple, ISBN 1-55945-204-8

Order today from your local Christian bookstore, or write: Group Publishing, P.O. Box 485, Loveland, CO 80539.